LEADERSHIP
ER

A Health Checkup
for You and Your Team

S TEPHEN F. KREMPL

CornerStone
Leadership Institute

www.**cornerstoneleadership**.com

Leadership ER

A Health Checkup for You and Your Team

Inquiries regarding permission for use of the material contained in this book should be addressed to:

CornerStone Leadership Institute
P.O. Box 764087
Dallas, TX 75376
888.789.LEAD

Printed in the United States of America
ISBN: 0-9746403-9-5

Credits

Consultant and Contributing Editor	Juli Baldwin, The Baldwin Group, Dallas, TX info@BaldwinGrp.com
Editor	Brenda Quinn, The Baldwin Group
Illustrator	Ashley Peck, The Baldwin Group
Design, art direction, and production	Melissa Monogue, Back Porch Creative, Plano, TX info@BackPorchCreative.com

Acknowledgments

I would like to start by thanking the numerous people I have had the honor to work with and who have had a profound influence on me over the years. Through my experiences with you, I have come to realize that many issues, concerns and challenges are common to all of us and cross geographic, cultural and economic boundaries.

I would also like to thank the many friends and colleagues who contributed to this project and provided feedback during the development of the book: Michael Roberts, Harmit Singh, Lai Kwok Kin, Laletha Nithiyanandan, Eliza Quek, John Bittleston, Hermann Ditzig, Tom Boldry, Mark Wilson, Chris Fulbright, Beverly Forte and Roger Krempl. I would also like to acknowledge Dr. Boyd Lyles, Jr., who co-authored our preceding book *Business ER*.

A very special thanks to Juli Baldwin for her invaluable contributions in shaping the ideas presented here and for editing the book. To David Holland, M.D. and Paul Fearneyhough, M.D., thank you for your review of the material and your input on the medical aspects of the book.

And to my family – my wife, Levirina, and my daughters Rachel, Chelsea, and Brittney – thank you for supporting me and this project.

Preface

Every minute of every day, someone – somewhere in the world – experiences a crisis. For some, it is a personal health crisis. For others, the crisis is at work, in their professional lives. Either way, *it changes their lives forever.*

The inspiration for *Leadership ER* was a catalytic personal health scare and the discovery that our personal lives often parallel our professional lives. These parallels are true across all geographic, cultural and economic boundaries.

Why do we experience similar fates in our personal and professional lives? I believe it is because it takes the same skills to run our personal lives as it does to run a department or team. The common denominator is *you* and how you frame your approach.

The connections between personal and business health are worth an examination, and that is what this book is about. Written as a story, it shares valuable insights on how to achieve and maintain personal health, business health, and the critical balance between the two.

I challenge you to discover how you can apply these insights to your own life by answering the questions at the end of each chapter. Use *Leadership ER* to help you develop an action plan to improve your health and the health of your team or department. Your willingness to stop, reflect and assess where you are can be a springboard to a new beginning of personal and professional health and vitality.

I hope this book will make a difference to you and to those who love you.

Stephen F. Krempl

Contents

1   THE COST OF DOING NOTHING

> *Don't wait for a major crisis to discover what is truly important.*

It was, without a doubt, the worst morning I had experienced in years.

I'd spent the previous night in turmoil, tossing and turning while Lynda slept peacefully beside me. I'd tried counting sheep and every other known farm animal, and I'd spent hours watching the ceiling fan blades slice the air. But no matter what I did, the voices in my head wouldn't let me sleep.

"Mike! Why didn't you tell us about these product problems?" shouted the fuming senior executives.

"Mike! Why didn't you tell us that management had moved up the project deadline?" yelled my irate team members.

"Mike! Why do your products have so many defects?" complained our customers.

As I flipped and flopped and tried to stop the voices, I worried that my career was doomed.

The whole episode had started yesterday afternoon with a phone call from my boss, Carmen.

"Mike, we need to talk," she'd begun. I detected something ominous in her tone, and I sat up and listened more closely.

"Sure, Carmen, what's up?" I said breezily, even though my heart pounded.

"You and I need to meet. How about tomorrow at 4:00? Does that work for you?"

"Works for me," I said, my stomach dropping with every passing second. "Uh, can I ask what this is about?"

"I think it's time we discussed the problem in your department."

"Oh," I cringed. Exactly which problem was she referring to – the missed deadlines? The fall in productivity? The product defects? Or the employee morale that was so low it was below freezing?

"Uh, do you want to see numbers? Should I print some reports?"

"Not necessary," she said. "Just bring yourself. I'll see you tomorrow at 4."

"Carmen, can I ask…"

"Sorry, Mike, I have to take another call. We'll talk tomorrow."

Since then, the meeting was all I could think about. My guess was that I was about to be fired. I'd tried to solve the problems in my department without involving Carmen, but obviously she'd found out about them somehow. Someone must have told her how bad things were.

I should have known I couldn't hide the problems forever – especially not after we'd had to issue the product recall four months ago. A recall was the last thing the company needed – we were already having financial problems. Not long ago, senior management had called a meeting for all middle managers and had laid it out for us: sales were way down and costs were way up. The company was bleeding red ink. In the words of our CEO, "Major restructuring will be required to return us to profitability."

My team members had obviously caught wind of the dire situation, because they kept asking me about the rumors: Were layoffs coming? Was it true the company was for sale?

In fact, just last week, one of my team leaders had cornered me in the elevator. "Mike, should I be looking for another job?" he'd asked. *Yeah*, I'd wanted to say. *Yeah, what you've heard is true. They really are talking about selling our division.* But I couldn't tell him that. I didn't know what to say to him. So I'd said nothing.

I guess I wasn't really surprised that morale in my department was at an all-time low. It seemed team members were always arguing over minor details and complaining about petty issues. Combine those problems with budget freezes and constant interdepartmental fights over resource allocations, and we had a real mess. Our missed deadlines had affected other departments' timelines, which had led to quality issues, which in turn had led to the recall.

For months I'd tried every management strategy I knew to solve our problems, but things weren't any better. And now I was going to get canned.

What else could the meeting be about? Everyone knows what kind of meetings happen late on Friday afternoons…especially when it's just you and your boss.

As I lay there in bed, I could picture the scene:

"We're letting you go, Mike," Carmen would say. Then some guy from security would walk me back to my desk, watch me as I cleaned it out, take my employee ID card, office keys and parking card, and walk me to the front door.

The worst part would be facing Lynda.

"I got fired," I'd say, choking on the words.

"Oh, Mike!" she'd sob. "What are we going to do? How will we pay the mortgage?"

We'd try to hide the stress from the kids, and we'd cut expenses here and there as I hunted for a job. But who'd want to hire a 46-year-old manager who'd been fired? I'd be permanently and chronically unemployed. Goodbye, middle class lifestyle.

I flipped and flopped some more. This couldn't be happening! Where had it all gone wrong?

■   ■   ■   ■   ■

Around 5:30, I just gave up on sleep. It was just before sunrise, and the gray pre-dawn light seeped through the bedroom curtains. The clock glared at me, ticking off the minutes until the dreaded meeting later that afternoon with Carmen. I had to get up in an hour anyway – I had to get into the office and prepare for the meeting. If I was going to have any chance of saving my job, I had to have answers. Unfortunately, all I had were questions.

As I crawled from the bed, I was stunned by a sudden, splitting headache. My temples throbbed with pain, and it felt as if a cold knitting needle had been jabbed into the center of my skull. No stranger to headaches, I kept a generous supply of over-the-counter migraine pain reliever stashed in various locations – in the bedside table, in the cabinet in the master bath, in the kitchen, in my car… and, of course, in my desk at work.

I dug through the drawer in the dark feeling for the bottle of pain reliever. I reached over to turn on the lamp, but my right arm wouldn't cooperate. It was numb and tingling. Asleep, I thought. My arm is asleep.

I tried to move it again, but it felt heavy, like a piece of lead. I wiggled my fingers. I could see them moving at the end of my hand, but they felt strange – as if they were on someone else's hand. As I struggled to make a fist, the pain in my head surged, and I winced.

I was on a mission to find that bottle of pain reliever. I fingered the contents of the drawer until finally I found it. Now for some water. It took all the strength I had to stand up and head toward the bathroom. My body felt as if it weighed a thousand pounds. Sleep... I just needed some sleep. Just too tired, I thought as I yawned a big wide yawn.

In the bathroom, I had trouble getting my right hand to shake out two pain reliever capsules. I decided I'd better take three instead – it was going to be one of those days.

Coffee. Heavy-duty, fully leaded, coffee-house coffee. Double shot, in fact. That's what I needed to shake this sleepiness.

I retraced my steps back to the bedroom. Every step was a chore, like climbing a mountain at high altitude. Partway to the closet, I was so tired I had to stop for a minute. As I stood there, leaning against the wall in the fading darkness, I felt all my strength suddenly drain out of me, and I nearly dropped to the ground.

"I *cannot* be sick today!" I muttered between clenched teeth, reaching for the doorframe to steady myself. I had to get ready for that meeting with Carmen. I needed to review the recall reports for the past three months and take a look at those trends. I had to talk to Kim and Isaac and get updates on their projects. And I had to put something together for Carmen outlining all the proactive ways I'd tried to resolve the issues in my department. I had to convince her we were making progress – I just needed more time to get things straightened out.

In the closet, I had to squint the light was so bright. I shuffled to the back of the closet to the chest of drawers. Just pulling the drawer open was an effort. It was bizarre – the weak muscles, the slow movements. What was going on? I'd heard that stress can cause physical problems, but this was ridiculous. I didn't have time for this.

As I emerged from the closet, I saw Lynda standing in the bathroom doorway. "Good morning," she said with a cheery lilt, wiping sleep from her eyes.

"Goo' mooorning, hunney. Cooo' yooo maeke me ah baagul?" The words were drawn and slurred as they rolled off my tongue. What was that? My mouth wasn't working much better than the rest of my body.

"What?" Lynda looked at me with curious concern. "Mike, sweetheart, are you all right?" She touched my shoulder and followed me into the bathroom. I felt like one of those walking zombies in a bad B movie. Taking a shower was going to be quite an experience.

"Ahhm fiyne, reeelly." Why couldn't I speak? I let loose a string of expletives in my head. If I couldn't talk, how would I be able to convince Carmen to give me another chance? Just then another wave of debilitating weakness washed over me. I reached out to steady myself against the bathroom counter, but my numb right arm gave way. I slipped a bit and put out my left arm to stop myself from falling.

"Mike," Lynda's voice was firm. "You're scaring me. Something is definitely wrong." I knew by the tone in her voice there was no way she was going to let me walk out of the house this morning. "We're going to the hospital."

"No," I said, and that word came out right. "Ahy have an imporrrnannt meeting thishafternoon."

Lynda bristled visibly. "I don't care about your meeting," she snapped. "That department can run for one day without you – we're going to the hospital."

Lynda helped me to the edge of the bed so I could sit down.

Then, with a whirl of her nightgown and a flurry of activity, she zipped into the closet and emerged fully clothed in T-shirt and jeans. Even with my head pounding, I knew that was the fastest I'd ever seen her get dressed. She knelt down and pulled on her shoes, looking up at me with wide eyes of concern. Although I had to admit I was feeling awful, it certainly didn't seem bad enough to warrant a trip to the hospital. I just needed to sleep for a few hours and give the pain reliever time to kick in. Then I'd be fine and I'd head to the office. I started to protest, "Lynnnda..."

She shot me one of those "don't test me" looks she gives the kids, and I knew there was no use arguing with her. Through the haze of pain in my head, I pictured Carmen sitting in the meeting room, tapping her pen on the tabletop, glancing up at the clock... waiting for me.

I tried a different approach. "But whutabou' the keeds?"

She thought for a minute. "I don't want to wake them. It might scare them to see you like this. I'll call Jan. I'm sure she wouldn't mind coming over and getting them off to school."

Lynda seemed determined to go to the hospital. I sat on the bed as she called our neighbor and good friend, Jan. I could hear Lynda talking fast, telling Jan what was happening, but her voice sounded far off. Then Lynda helped me dress. It made me feel like a child, but I could barely function. On second thought, maybe Lynda was right...maybe going to the hospital wasn't such a bad idea after all.

By the time we made our way downstairs to the car, Jan was there. She assured us she'd take care of Josh and Rachel and told us not to worry. As Lynda stepped into the car, I thought about my laptop. Surely I'd feel better in a bit – I had to. This couldn't be anything serious. And there we'd be, sitting in the waiting room for hours with nothing to do. If I had the laptop, I could use the time to work on that list for Carmen. I tried to get the words out to ask Lynda to grab the computer.

She turned to look at me, her face serious, as she punched the garage door opener. I couldn't tell if she didn't understand what I had said or if she just decided to ignore me.

■   ■   ■   ■   ■

We drove in silence for a few miles. Then Lynda gently asked, "Honey, these symptoms have been getting worse, haven't they?"

"I dunno."

I stared out the window. She was right – the symptoms had been getting worse but I didn't want to admit it. About a year ago, I'd started getting simple tension headaches. But over time, the headaches got worse – so much so that I went to see the doctor. He diagnosed them as migraines and pointed out that I hadn't had a physical exam in eight years. Since I'd just turned 45, I figured a checkup was probably a good idea. Big mistake! The next thing I knew, the doctor had prescribed medication for high blood pressure and recommended exercise and a change of diet.

That was a year ago, and the headaches weren't any better. I just made sure I always had plenty of migraine medicine around. Of course I hadn't exactly followed the doctor's recommendations. I hadn't taken the blood pressure medication, wasn't exercising more, and hadn't made much effort to change my diet. The bottom line was, I hadn't done anything to improve my health.

Then a few months ago, I started noticing that occasionally my right hand would tingle and feel numb. I hadn't thought much of it, but now I was beginning to wonder if I should have paid more attention. Maybe I should have gone to the doctor and had it checked out.

"We've got to make sure you're taking care of this, Mike," Lynda said. Then she added, almost to herself, "We're going to have to make a plan and stick to it if things are going to get better."

"Yur rieght," I agreed. "Ahhyneeed to fallowuup..."

As we drove, I leaned back and closed my eyes, and before long my thoughts turned to work. Despite the headache and fogginess in my brain, it slowly dawned on me that the problems at work had been getting worse over time also. When I'd first taken over my department, I'd inherited a few challenges but nothing really serious. I didn't have any experience as a new leader in an existing department (I had always been promoted up through the ranks), so I'd asked a fellow operations manager for advice. He'd given me some good ideas – team goals, action plans, project updates, weekly team meetings, etc. – but I never followed up and implemented any of them. I guess I got distracted by the daily "to do's" and lost sight of the long-term plan.

Needless to say, the problems had only gotten worse. What had started out as a few minor issues had ballooned into a full-blown crisis. Looking back, I could see there had been signs that the situation was deteriorating, but I'd ignored them – along with the suggestions from my colleague – just as I'd ignored my physical symptoms and the recommendations from my doctor. I'd been in denial about the problems with my team just like I'd been in denial about my health problems.

As we neared the hospital, Lynda slowed down. She pulled into the entrance marked "Emergency" and turned off the car. "Sit there," she said, and she ran around to my side of the car to help me out. "Don't worry, honey. We're going to get you help." Her voice was full of emotion.

I couldn't bear to look her in the eye. "Ahhyshoulnnn't 'ave waaited soolong."

I'd been warned, but I'd done nothing to improve my health or the situation with my team, and now I was paying the price. What would be the ultimate cost?

"Ahhy'ope isssnot too late."

A TIME TO REFLECT

The Cost of Doing Nothing

It took a crisis in Mike's life for him to pause long enough to reflect and gain some insight. Now is the time for you to learn from Mike's story and avoid a crisis of your own. Invest the time to answer the questions below and at the end of each of the following chapters. Stop, reflect and assess where you are and what actions you can take to improve your health and the health of your team or department.

Personal Health

♦ What symptoms do you recognize that could be early warning signs of an impending health crisis?

♦ What health problems or potential health problems (that you know of) are you in denial about?

♦ What will it take to motivate you to get these symptoms checked out by a doctor?

♦ What are the potential costs of doing nothing – of ignoring your health problems?

Business Health

♦ What symptoms do you recognize that could be early warning signs of an impending crisis in your department or with your team?

♦ What business problems or potential problems (that you know of)
are you in denial about?

♦ What will it take to motivate you to check out these situations
and find out more about them?

♦ What are the potential costs of doing nothing – of ignoring the
problems with your team or in your department?

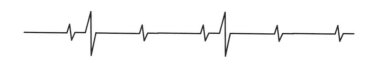

2 THE FEAR OF NOT KNOWING

> "Nothing in life is to be feared.
> It is only to be understood."
>
> – Marie Curie

Lynda was right by my side as an orderly whisked me through the ER doors in a wheelchair. We went past the front desk, down a tiled hallway, and into a small, cold room.

The controlled but intense activity of the ER was overwhelming. Two nurses helped me from the wheelchair to a gurney and removed my shirt. One nurse started oxygen through a nasal canula and then took my vital signs. Another nurse came in and deftly hooked me up to a heart monitor. Still another started an IV.

We hadn't been in the room more than a few minutes when a doctor entered. "I'm Dr. Garcia. How are you doing, Mike?"

"Ahhm havinggshum poblems."

"Just relax, we're going to help you," he quickly reassured me. He asked several questions about my symptoms and then performed what he called a "brief neurological exam."

"I'm ordering a complete blood workup," he said. "And once your condition stabilizes a bit more, we're going to do some additional tests, including an EKG and a chest x-ray. Then we'll take a look at everything and see what we've got. I'll be back in a bit. Okay?"

I nodded and Lynda said, "Thank you."

One of the nurses turned to Lynda, "You're his wife?"

"Yes."

"I need to get a brief medical history on him," she said. Lynda told her how I'd been diagnosed with migraines and high blood pressure last year and that the doctor had prescribed medicine and recommended a change in diet and more exercise.

"Did he take the medicine as prescribed?"

"Not really," Lynda said, cringing. "We didn't follow up too well. And instead of losing weight, he's actually gained about 15 pounds."

"And what about the exercise?"

"Well, golf is about the only exercise he gets…"

"So the cart probably gets the best workout, right?" The nurse smiled at me, but I could tell she wasn't impressed.

"Does he smoke?"

"He quit about 10 years ago."

"What are some of the recent problems he's experienced?"

"Well," Lynda answered, "about two months ago he began complaining that the headaches were more severe…"

"Nummmmness innmy hand," I added.

"Numbness in your hand?" the nurse asked.

I nodded.

"Then today, he woke up with slurred speech and could barely move his right hand and arm. And his headache was really bad again. I decided to bring him in."

"You did the right thing bringing him in," said the nurse as she wrote on my chart.

"Mike's father died of a stroke 10 years ago…he was only 58," Lynda said slowly. She looked at me, and I saw the fear in her eyes.

Then I got scared too.

"And how old is Mike?"

"46."

"AhmI havvvina stroke?" I tried to ask.

"That's what we're going to find out," said the nurse. "Right now I need you to relax. The doctor will be back in a minute to talk with you."

A stroke. Just hearing the word filled me with a sense of dread. A stroke could kill me, just like it did Dad. Why hadn't I thought about Dad before? I reached out and took Lynda's hand.

She squeezed my hand and whispered, "Hang in there, honey."

Lynda stared at the heart monitor…I stared up at the ceiling. This was serious. How did it come to this? Why hadn't I seen it coming?

Of course, I knew the answer. All the signs had been there – I'd just ignored them. Hearing Lynda tell my story, I felt like an idiot. I mean, with that kind of family history and those symptoms, who'd ignore a doctor's advice? Why hadn't I done something?

Because there wasn't enough time. There were all my responsibilities at home, plus my commitment as a board member for a local non-profit organization. And of course, there was work. There was just always something else that seemed more important. And yet here I was, facing possible termination – of both my life and my job!

And then I remembered my meeting with Carmen. "Lynna, canu calll Carmen a'thoffice, tell'er ahmmnoty goinna make itinn for ar meeetng?" I struggled just to get the words out.

"Okay, sweetheart. I'll be right back." And she disappeared down the hall.

I laid quietly on the gurney and closed my eyes. I hated not knowing the cause of my symptoms, yet I dreaded finding out what it was. Once I knew, I'd have to take responsibility and do something about it. Inaction had always been one of my weaknesses. Yeah, I was a procrastinator. Why do today what can be put off until tomorrow? Now I wasn't so sure there would even be a tomorrow.

Please, I prayed, *let there be a tomorrow. I swear I'll take this seriously and take responsibility for my health. Just give me one more chance to do things right.*

■   ■   ■   ■   ■

Lynda seemed more relaxed when she came back. "I talked to Carmen and told her what's going on. She said you can reschedule the meeting when you get back. She's going to meet with your team. She seems to think Kim and Isaac can keep things running while you're out. She seemed really concerned and wanted me to tell you to just concentrate on your health and getting better."

I nodded my head but my stomach dropped. Oh great! She was already thinking about who would replace me. This would give her a chance to see Kim and Isaac in action, to see if they could run the department.

Just thinking about work brought back that familiar knot of stress. It was frustrating not knowing why things were going so badly. As far as I could tell, I did all the same things the other department heads did, but they got far better results. I worked long hours and kept close tabs on people and projects. But I couldn't figure out the root cause of all the problems, let alone know how to fix them.

Of course, if I did know what was causing the problems, I'd have to do something about it. Back to those issues of responsibility and procrastination again. There was another parallel between my personal health issues and my department's problems. I knew there was an important connection in all of this, but I hadn't yet figured out exactly what it was.

■　■　■　■　■

"How are you feeling, Mike?" asked Dr. Garcia as he walked into the room. He looked serious. That couldn't be good.

I just shrugged. My head was pounding, and I still felt very weak, not to mention harried from all the commotion.

"He still can't speak very well," said Lynda.

"All right. Well, the initial series of diagnostics hasn't given us much to go on. We didn't find any problem with the blood work. Likewise, the EKG and chest x-ray didn't reveal any indication of a problem. However, your blood pressure is dangerously high, and that will definitely need to be addressed. We still don't know what's causing your symptoms. So we're going to run a few more tests, including a CAT scan. We just want to make sure we've looked at every possibility before recommending treatment."

"What does a CAT scan check for?" Lynda asked.

"It will show us if there's any bleeding in the brain from a stroke. It would also reveal a brain tumor."

A brain tumor? It hit me again just how serious this was – it hit me hard in the chest like a tangible force.

My palms began to sweat. I could feel my heart pounding and my chest tightening. I suddenly felt sick to my stomach. As I moved my head, a stabbing pain ran down the back of my neck, shot through my arm and surged deep into my chest. With each breath, my chest seemed to constrict more. Oh God, this was it! A heart attack! My whole body went cold with fear.

"Thocter," I gasped, "I thunk ahmI havvvin a poblem."

Dr. Garcia must have read the fear in my face, because he immediately checked my pulse rate against the second hand of his watch. "Just calm down, Mike. Take a few slow, deep breaths for me. That's it, relax."

I looked up at Lynda and saw her eyes filling with tears. She reached out and rubbed my shoulder. I realized something important in that moment: All the time that I'd been obsessing about myself and my job, Lynda had been faithfully by my side. She was my cornerstone – she and the kids meant everything to me. And yet, each day I was completely wrapped up in the constant blanket of troubles at work.

And now I was going to die. I'd never be able to make it up to her.

Dr. Garcia's voice brought me back. "Mike, you're having a panic attack. I understand you're anxious, but try to relax. Take some more deep breaths. I'm going to admit you to the hospital and ask a neurologist to come down for a consultation, okay?"

All I could do was nod. A neurologist? That had to mean there was something seriously wrong. What if they couldn't find the cause of the problem? What if I died before they found out what was wrong? I decided right then that fear and uncertainty was definitely worse than facing reality, accepting responsibility, and doing something about it.

"We'll get it figured out," said Dr. Garcia as if he had read my mind. "We're narrowing it down. It'll just take some time. Just hang tight and have patience."

The doctor's assurances didn't make me feel any better. Why couldn't they figure out what was wrong? Once again, I reached out for Lynda.

"It's going to be all right, honey," she whispered. "We'll get through this." She sounded like she was trying to convince herself as well.

But I wasn't convinced. Was it really going to be all right...or was this the end?

A TIME TO REFLECT

The Fear of Not Knowing

Mike missed several opportunities to improve his personal and team health. He ignored his family history and didn't follow through on earlier recommendations made by his doctor. Now, it could cost him his life. And his refusal to address the problems with his team could cost him his job. He failed to accept the fact that his health, and the health of his department, are his responsibility, and his alone. Answer the following questions to discover some opportunities to improve your health.

Personal Health

♦ Do you know of any illnesses that you are at risk of developing because of family history or current lifestyle?

♦ Are you aware of the warning signs and symptoms of the illnesses you are at risk of developing?

♦ What action can you take to prevent these potential health problems?

♦ What are you doing in the areas of diet, exercise and stress to improve your overall health?

Business Health

♦ What issues or problems did you inherit when you took over your current leadership position?

♦ What problems or mistakes do you see your organization or department repeating?

♦ What mechanism is in place to detect patterns that can be indicators of future problems?

♦ How will you track and address potential problems?

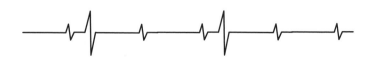

3 THE SEARCH FOR ANSWERS

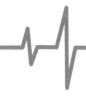

> *"As long as one keeps searching, the answers come."*
>
> – Joan Baez

"Hello, Mike. I'm Dr. Lee, the neurologist. And you must be Lynda." A tall woman with a no-nonsense air swept into the room and shook our hands. "Are you feeling any better?"

"Ahm feeling allittle better." My speech was starting to clear up some, too.

"And how's your arm?"

"Starting to get some feellingain."

"Good. That means you're headed in the right direction. The CAT scan Dr. Garcia ran was inconclusive. So I'd like to do an MRI and an ultrasound to follow up on a possible stroke or mini-stroke. The MRI will show the brain in finer detail than the CAT scan. Unfortunately, it will probably be tomorrow morning before I have the results. You get some rest tonight. All right?"

I nodded, "Okay."

■   ■   ■   ■   ■

A short time later, a nurse stopped in and asked if she could check my vitals and draw some more blood.

I was starting to feel like a lab rat, but I nodded in agreement. What choice did I have? You have to run tests if you want answers. I watched as the nurse inserted the needle into my arm, and the glass collection tube began to fill with blood. There's information in that blood, I thought. That information will be taken to the lab where experts will look at it, draw some conclusions, and make a report.

Checking vital signs. Gathering information. My mind wandered back to work again. Sitting there with the needle stuck in my arm, I decided that in many ways, an organization is like the human body. And like a body, its health and well-being depend on how well it's kept in shape. Every so often it needs a checkup and its vital signs need monitoring. Yeah, I liked that comparison…until I thought about it some more.

When was the last time my department had a checkup? I couldn't remember. Was anyone checking its vital signs? I sure wasn't.

Maybe that's why my department was in the ER…just like I was.

I was certain that finding all these parallels between work and the ER was just a way for me to cope with the stress of my situation. Obviously, my work issues were relatively minor compared to strokes and brain tumors and death. But the parallels were fascinating and they gave me better insight into the problems at work. And of course, the harder I looked the more similarities I found.

As the nurse finished drawing my blood, an orderly showed up to take me to another part of the hospital for the MRI and ultrasound. As he wheeled me down the corridors, I noticed other people moving slowly through the hallways. Many of them seemed to be in worse shape than me. How many of them had known a crisis was coming – a crisis that would shut down the entire operation of their normal lives?

It also occurred to me that just as there were lots of people in worse shape than me, there were probably lots of businesses out there that were in as bad or worse shape than the one I worked for. It was another correlation. Maybe I was desperate to put a positive spin on my circumstances, but I felt like everything that was happening to me held a valuable lesson – something to be learned, not only for my own health, but also for my team's benefit. I decided I'd try to find as many connections as possible between the two situations. It had to be better than dwelling on the uncertainty of my health.

■ ■ ■ ■ ■

I closed my eyes and listened to the rhythm of the MRI machine. The seriousness of the situation weighed on me, and I tried to stay calm. This is all just information, I kept reminding myself. They're just gathering information so they can find the answer. They're being thorough.

My thoughts drifted back and forth between my ordeal here at the hospital and the one at the office. Had I gathered enough information to find the solution to our problems? Had I been thorough enough? Unfortunately, the answer on both counts was no.

My thoughts turned back to Lynda, and guilt nagged at me as I realized how steadfast she had been in the face of this potential tragedy. She was always there for me when I needed her most.

Loyalty. That was a big issue at work these days! Was my team loyal to me? I didn't know. Maybe there was a more important question: was I loyal to them? I was ashamed when I had to answer no. During these last difficult months, I'd been more concerned about myself than about the people on my team. The truth was, I hadn't been there when they needed me the most – when rumors were swirling about finances, layoffs and buyouts.

■   ■   ■   ■   ■

After the MRI, the orderly wheeled me to the ultrasound lab on another floor of the hospital. The technician explained that she'd look at my heart and the carotid arteries, the main arteries in the neck that supply blood to the brain.

She started at my neck, examining each carotid artery, moving the probe up and down, taking pictures as she went along. Then she moved on to the heart. The ultrasound picked up the slurping-sucking sounds of my heartbeat and amplified them in the room. As the technician looked at my heart from a number of different views, I watched it pulsating on the screen. It was strange watching this life-giving organ do its work. Here was something that had such great importance to my life, and yet I didn't understand how it worked.

As the minutes dragged on, I let my mind wander. Was there another connection here – some situation at work I could compare this to? What about all those reports? How many times had I looked at reports that I didn't fully understand and yet were so critical to the well-being and survival of my department? How many times had I set them aside, thinking someone else must be on top of it? Probably too many to count.

■   ■   ■   ■   ■

After the MRI and ultrasound, the orderly wheeled me to a private room where Lynda was waiting. The room was quiet, comfortable and had a television, which helped to take my mind off things for a while. Thankfully, I was finally feeling better. The numbness in my arm and hand was gone, my speech was almost back to normal, and I had only a slight headache. I hadn't been in the new room long when I heard a familiar voice.

"Hey, Mike. Are you up for a visitor?"

"Tom!" I was surprised to see him. "Come on in. What are you doing here?"

"Well, I heard from Carmen that you were rushed to the ER this morning and that you were still in the hospital. I decided I had to come check on you myself. How are you? What's going on?"

He gave Lynda a big, reassuring hug, then walked over and put his hand on my shoulder. Tom was a close friend and just an all-around good guy. He's one of those rare people who genuinely cares about other people and takes the time to show it.

Tom and I met at work, and we quickly became good friends. When I hired on at the company, he was the controller. He had started out as an entry-level accounting clerk and worked his way up through the ranks, and now he was next in line for the CFO position. Tom was definitely a rising star.

Unlike some other leaders, Tom always remembered what it was like to be a team member working in the trenches. And I was certain that when he became the CFO, he wouldn't forget what it was like to be a mid-level leader. He once told me that middle managers play a critical role in the organization: "We are the bridges between employees and senior management," he'd said. "Our primary responsibilities are to clearly articulate management's vision to employees, and to act as a conduit for employees to convey critical information about the business up to senior management."

I found Tom to be a valuable sounding board. Every so often he and I would get together to bounce ideas off one another and help each other with different leadership problems – although it seemed that I always came away from our sessions having received more help than I'd given. In fact, months ago Tom had suggested some solutions for my department. But like the recommendations from my doctor, those suggestions never made it to the top of my priority list.

Lynda gave Tom a quick run-down on the day's events. When she finished, she asked, "Tom, would you mind staying with Mike for a few hours? I don't want to leave him alone, but I really need to run home and check on the kids and arrange for someone to stay with them tonight."

"Lynda, I don't need a babysitter," I complained, embarrassed. "I'm in the hospital – there are plenty of people around."

"I know. I'd just feel better if someone was here in the room with you," she said.

"It's not a problem. I'd be happy to," Tom interjected. "We'll watch the baseball game."

I was too tired to argue. Besides, I wanted to find out from Tom what was going on at work.

"Oh, Lynda," I said as she was walking out the door, "would you please bring my laptop when you come back tonight?"

She turned and looked at me, mouth open, her disbelief apparent. "How can you be worried about work at a time like this?"

"Please, honey. It's important to me. It'll help me keep my mind off of...all of this. And besides, I need to check my email."

"Oh, all right," she said reluctantly.

After Lynda left, Tom wanted to know more about my situation. So I filled him in on everything, from waking up with the symptoms this morning to the tests they'd been running to try and identify the problem. And I told him how I'd found all these connections between my health and my situation at work with my team.

"I know you've been under a lot of stress at work lately," he said.

"Do you think that's what brought this on?"

"Stress! You don't know the half of it. First, on Wednesday, Carmen asked me for the most recent management reports for my department. I told her it would take me a few days to pull them together. Then she called yesterday and asked for them again – said she had to have them today."

"What's the significance of that?"

"Carmen's never asked for all my reports, let alone asked twice. Something is definitely up. And then, she asked to meet with me this afternoon. I think I'm on my way out the door." I tried to keep the emotion out of my voice, but it was hard not to be dejected.

"I'd be shocked if she let you go," said Tom, the surprise evident on his face. "I don't think she'd do that without giving you some kind of warning and a chance to solve the problems."

"But that's just it. I'm not even sure what's causing the problems. In fact, it's a lot like what's going on with my health. I don't know what's wrong in either area, and it's incredibly frustrating."

"But didn't you say the doctors are running some tests to determine what's causing your symptoms?" he asked.

"Yeah. A bunch of tests!"

"Have you gotten the results back yet?"

"A few," I said. "The EKG didn't really show anything. Neither did the CAT scan. This afternoon they did an MRI to look at the blood vessels in the brain and an ultrasound to see if there's any blockage in the carotid artery. I won't have those results back until tomorrow morning."

"So they're running multiple tests? One test wouldn't have been enough to get an accurate diagnosis?"

"That's right."

"So why can't you use the same process at work to diagnose the problems in your department?" he asked.

His comment caught me off guard, and I paused for a moment. Tom had a way of getting to the heart of the matter and asking questions that made me think. "What do you mean?" I asked hesitantly.

"Well, you just told me you were drawing parallels between your health and your work, so let's draw a few more. Just like in healthcare, we use tests in business to help us diagnose problems. The consultants call them metrics, right? They help us understand what's happening in the organization by highlighting problems and issues, and identifying the root causes of problems. Metrics are the results or output of audits, financial statements, customer satisfaction surveys, focus groups, climate surveys, 360° profiles, balance score cards, Six Sigma Scores, and so on, and so on, and..."

I smiled. "Okay. I see what you're getting at. So just like the doctors are running some tests on me, I could use a couple of metrics to get some answers at work."

"Well, there's a danger in only doing one or two tests," Tom said, a note of caution in his voice. "Basing decisions on limited information can cause us to misdiagnose the problem. We have to see the whole picture if we want valid answers."

"I'm about to lose my job, Tom – I don't have time for that kind of testing. Plus, it seems like overkill to run all the metrics you just mentioned."

"You're right – you can have too many," Tom answered. "When that happens, we tend to get overwhelmed and not use any of them. Too few and too many – both are problems. It takes a combination of carefully chosen metrics to give us a clear picture so we can make an accurate diagnosis."

"So let's assume I run some diagnostics and identify the problem. Then what?" I asked.

"You have to be certain you've thoroughly analyzed the situation before moving ahead with a solution," Tom said. "If the doctor discovered a spot on your chest x-ray, you wouldn't want him to do surgery without doing some more investigating, right? Sometimes, a particular metric will indicate a potential problem, but we don't bother to get more information. If a problem exists, we need to do more testing to uncover the details and causes. For example, the sales report might show that sales are still up, but customer metrics are trending down, potentially having a negative effect on future sales. That's when we need to dig deeper to find out the 'why' behind the customer metrics.

"On the other hand, sometimes we spend a lot of energy assessing the cause of a problem, but then we don't invest the time, money or resources to make the needed changes," Tom continued. "We don't follow through with action. It's kind of like filling a prescription and not taking the medication."

"I know all about that one," I smiled sheepishly.

"Now let me ask you another question: Who reviews and interprets your medical test results?"

"The doctors, of course." That was a rather odd question, I thought.

"Someone who is specifically trained to read the results and interpret them correctly, right?"

"Well, yeah. I wouldn't want just anyone diagnosing me."

"Exactly. But we frequently make that mistake in business. Oftentimes our metrics are so complex they're difficult to understand, but we don't call in experts with training and experience to help us interpret them. We managers get the reports, look them over and make our own interpretations. But different people can draw different conclusions from the same set of data. Truth be told, there are plenty of times when I'm not certain what to do with the information I get from a report."

I laughed. "Man, am I glad to hear you say that! I thought I was the only one."

"Imagine how valuable that information would be to us as leaders if we knew exactly how to interpret and apply the results – like the doctor interpreting the results of your tests. What if HR explained the meaning behind the results of the recent climate survey? Or if I, as the controller, sat down with department managers and helped them understand how the financial statements specifically relate to their departments? Or if Gary, the VP of Sales, were to explain why sales are down? What's the point in performing tests if no one reviews or applies the results?"

I nodded slowly. "You know, Tom, I have to fess up to something." I hadn't told anyone about this before. It was too embarrassing to admit that I'd dropped the ball. "Several months ago, I conducted a customer satisfaction survey with my department's internal customers. I tabulated the results, but then never did anything with the information. I didn't even communicate the results to my team. I wanted to follow up on the survey – I guess I just got caught up in other priorities. After a month or so, I felt like it was too late to do anything with it so I just filed it away."

Tom didn't criticize me. "We have the tools in business to accurately diagnose our problems, but we frequently don't use them to our full advantage. I have to admit, I'm guilty of that one too," Tom said, awkwardness creeping into his voice. "I haven't done anything with my 360° feedback for the last few years. I look it over, discuss it with my boss and put a plan together to address the developmental opportunities that come up, but then I don't take action on my plan. I know what I need to do, but I just don't do it."

"I guess I feel better knowing I'm not the only guilty one," I said. "It's a shame how often we conduct a survey, do an assessment or generate a report – or even worse, ask a team member to generate a report for us – and then do nothing with it. What kind of message does that send?"

It was a hypothetical question, but Tom answered it anyway. "It sends the message that the report wasn't really necessary, that the information provided wasn't important, and that the time of the person who generated the report isn't valuable."

"You're right," I said as I stifled a yawn. All this conversation had left me feeling exhausted.

"You need to get some rest," Tom said.

"I think I'll do that. I'm awfully tired all of a sudden. You can go home. I'll tell Lynda you did your duty," I smiled.

"There was no duty involved – you're my friend. I'm just glad you're all right. I'll stop by again tomorrow."

"Thanks for coming by, Tom. I never would have guessed today would be the day I'd make headway on this mess at work, but you've really helped me sort some things out. Let me just make sure I've got this right…

"I need to be the doctor for my department. I need to determine the right combination of tests that will diagnose our problems. But it's not the test results themselves that are most important – it's the *interpretation of the results* that's the key to an accurate diagnosis, and that may require some expert advice. If a test indicates a problem, I may need to perform additional tests or gather more information to fully understand the situation. Ultimately, I have to *do* something with the results – I have to take action – if my department is going to get healthy. How do you like those parallels?"

"I couldn't have said it better myself. Do you think that's

something you can do when you get back to work?"

"Absolutely."

■　■　■　■　■

I tried to rest, but sleep wouldn't come. At least I was feeling more confident about my abilities to resolve my problems at work. For the first time in many months, it seemed I had the beginnings of a workable plan that would help me uncover the cause of the problems in my department. There might yet be hope – maybe I could save my job after all.

I rolled over on my side and adjusted the pillow. Lying there in the silence without anything to distract me, all the worry and fear about my health came rushing back. I just wanted to know what was wrong with me so I could get on with fixing it. At least tomorrow I'd have the results of the MRI and ultrasound.

I also came to the sobering realization that all of the trauma and stress of recent months – and certainly the last 24 hours – could have been avoided. Months ago, when my headaches got worse and the numbness in my hand started, I should have gone back to the doctor for more tests. At work, I should have gone back and reviewed the results from the diagnostics I'd already conducted.

I hated to admit that I could have prevented both of these events if only I hadn't ignored the warning signs and symptoms. Why had it taken two major crises to realize that?

A TIME TO REFLECT

The Search for Answers

Solutions to problems – whether personal health problems or work problems – must be based on a complete and accurate diagnosis of the situation. Mike recognized that he couldn't take action until he knew the root cause of his symptoms. The questions below will encourage you to examine how you gather the information that will help you determine the causes of your challenges.

Personal Health

♦ Do you get regular checkups (appropriate to your age or medical condition) to review your current health condition and uncover potential problems?

♦ Do you conscientiously follow up on the results from your checkups?

♦ What can you do to prevent any deterioration of your current condition?

♦ Is there anything more you could be doing to improve your specific problem areas – smoking, poor diet, high blood pressure, sugar imbalance, high cholesterol, excessive weight, etc.?

♦ How do you stay current on information (i.e., new preventive medicines, procedures, techniques, etc.) about your specific health condition?

Business Health

♦ Do you conduct regular checkups of your organization or department to review the status of current problems and uncover new ones?

♦ How can you assess your team's condition and diagnose any problems?

♦ What "tests" can you run? How do you ensure that data and results are interpreted correctly?

♦ What measures can you take to keep current problems from worsening and prevent future problems from developing?

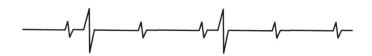

4

THE COMFORT
OF KNOWING

> *"There are no simple solutions. Only intelligent choices."*
>
> – Author Unknown

Early the next morning, Dr. Lee, the neurologist, walked into my room with some medical charts and papers tucked under her arm. Here we go, I thought. She has the results of the MRI and ultrasound – I'll finally know what's going on. I could feel my chest tightening.

"How are you feeling this morning?" she asked as she shook hands in a business-like manner.

"Other than not sleeping well last night, pretty much back to normal," I answered.

"Good. No numbness or headache this morning?"

"No – not at all." C'mon, I thought. Just get to the point.

"Well, I know this has been a long 24 hours for you. Let's go over these test results." She put on the glasses that were hanging around her neck.

"What did you find?" Lynda asked, tightening her grip on my hand.

"The MRI was clear – there was no evidence of a tumor or

bleeding in the brain from a stroke."

Thank God! Hearing those words sent a wave of relief through my body. The two things I'd feared most – a stroke and a tumor – were out of the picture. I was so busy celebrating I almost missed what she said next.

"But the ultrasound of your left carotid artery showed there is a partial blockage due to a buildup of plaque, and that is what caused your symptoms yesterday."

"What does that mean?" I asked.

"Basically, what you suffered yesterday is called a TIA – Transient Ischemic Attack. It's kind of a mini-stroke. Because of the blockage, the blood flow to your brain was temporarily interrupted, but then restored. The lack of blood flow creates a disturbance in the brain, causing it to stop communicating correctly with certain parts of the body. The result is headache, weakness or numbness, difficulty walking, and slurred speech. With a stroke, the neurological damage is usually permanent. However, with a TIA the symptoms occur and then disappear, usually within 24 hours, and the person returns to normal."

Maybe I'd celebrated too soon – a mini-stroke wasn't exactly good news. But I was feeling completely normal, so maybe it wasn't that big of a deal after all.

"But," Dr. Lee held up her hand, and I knew there was more to come. "TIAs should not be ignored, Mike. They are an important warning sign of a more serious stroke to come if we don't head off these problems right now."

"TIA," I said slowly, mulling it over. "How did this happen? I thought only older people have strokes. Obviously my father died of a stroke, but he was in his late 50s. I'm only 46."

"Actually, anyone can have a stroke, but there are certain groups that are more at risk. For example, men have strokes more frequently than women. Younger people, like you, tend to downplay or rationalize their symptoms or attribute them to something else. The number one risk factor for a stroke or TIA is high blood pressure. Other factors are diabetes, cardiac disease, smoking and high cholesterol. You have a number of the risk factors: You're a male, you have high blood pressure that has gone untreated, your cholesterol is quite a bit higher than it should be, and you're an ex-smoker." As she talked, she counted the risk factors on her fingers. "All of these contributed to the blockage." Four fingers. Four risk factors. Why hadn't I paid attention to those four things before?

Dr. Lee removed her glasses and looked me straight in the eye. "Again, I want to impress upon you that a TIA is a warning of a potentially more serious stroke if you don't make some changes to improve your risk factors." Her voice was serious, and I knew she meant business. Lynda and I exchanged looks.

"The good news is," her face and voice softened as she continued, "we know the cause of the problem. Now we just have to decide how to best treat it. Basically, you've got two options, but both carry some risks. The first is surgery to remove some of the blockage. But there is the potential for complications in performing a carotid endarterectomy. When we go in to clean out the buildup of plaque, some plaque could dislodge and cause another stroke."

"What's the other option?" So far I didn't like what I'd heard.

"The other option is to try some new medications and significant lifestyle changes, including diet and exercise."

"That sounds more like it," I said, with an attempt at a smile. "I can do that. I really don't like the thought of surgery." Surgery… cutting things out. Cutting *me* out – that's what Carmen was planning to do.

"Mike," she said, as she gave me another of her direct looks, "it's absolutely critical for you to understand that if you opt for the medications and lifestyle changes, you're going to have to do everything *exactly* as prescribed, or you almost certainly will have a stroke. And the next one may not be as forgiving."

"I get it," I said, nodding gravely. I swallowed hard. This was serious stuff. I was determined to really listen to the doctor this time.

"We'll have to wait to decide on treatment for a while yet," the doctor said. "We've got you scheduled for an angiogram later this morning to take a closer look at that blockage. That will tell us if you're a candidate for surgery. It may be necessary if there's some 'ratty' appearing plaque in there, or if the blockage exceeds 50 to 60 percent of the artery diameter. We'll take a look at the results of the angiogram, and then you'll have to make a decision. I'll let the two of you discuss it. I'll be back later this afternoon."

We were quiet for a minute. Lynda was the first to speak. "I don't like the idea of surgery either. But if you decide to try changing your diet and exercising, you really have to follow through this time, Mike. You heard what she said. You don't have any other choice."

"I know, and you're right." It was true – I didn't have any other choice this time. Not with my health and not with the health of my department. If I didn't follow through and make some changes, I might not have any more chances, personally or professionally.

■　■　■　■　■

Lynda went home to freshen up and spend some time with the kids. She'd mentioned that Josh seemed to be taking the entire situation in stride. Rachel, on the other hand, was upset. Lynda considered bringing them to the hospital to see me, but we both decided that might make matters worse. Hopefully I wouldn't be there long. When I got home, I'd spend some time with them. With everything going on at work, I hadn't spent time with my children in months. I missed them. When this was all over, I was going to have a lot of making up to do with them as well as with Lynda.

I was actually glad to have some time alone. I needed to think, to process everything that had happened over the last 24 hours.

Although it was difficult for me to accept that I'd had a TIA – especially at my age – I was relieved to finally know for certain what was wrong. But lying there in the hospital bed, it hit me square in the face that I was responsible for this situation – there was no one to blame except myself. If I had accepted responsibility for my health a lot sooner and followed the doctor's recommendations last year, this never would have happened. Or even if I had heeded the warning signs that had appeared over the last several months and taken steps then to make changes, this whole episode might still have been avoided.

There was a certain kind of comfort in knowing the truth… even if it was tough to face. I wondered if I would find the same comfort in finally knowing the cause of my problems at work. I was eager to get back and find out.

As I lay there, I went through everything Tom and I had talked about yesterday. I remembered what Tom had said about not taking action on his 360° feedback report, and it got me thinking about my own 360° feedback. Like Tom, I had looked at it but hadn't done much with the information. I couldn't remember many specifics from the report, but one thing stood out in my mind: the feedback from both my direct reports and my boss had clearly indicated that communication was one of my weaknesses.

At the time, I had been defensive about the feedback. Carmen had made comments before that I didn't keep her informed. And I suspected that the feedback from some of my team members was given in retaliation for some other issues. But now I realized I had simply been in denial. Obviously, if that many people thought I had a communication problem, I did. I wondered about the details behind the feedback. What was I doing – or not doing – that was creating a communication problem?

"You look better today," said a voice. I looked up to see Tom coming through the door.

"Better all the time, thanks," I smiled. "Couldn't stay away from this place, is that it?"

He laughed. "I can't get enough of that antiseptic smell."

Then I laughed.

"So how're things today? Any news?"

I told him what the neurologist had said about my condition, the possible treatments, and that the results of the angiogram would determine the best option.

"You seem relieved to have an answer," he said.

"Definitely. The uncertainty was the worst part."

"I agree. I hate being in the dark too. And it sounds like your doctor does a good job of communicating with you. It makes a big difference, doesn't it?"

Communication. There was that word again. "How did you know I was thinking about communication issues at work?"

"Hey, you're the one drawing the parallels," he chuckled. "Glad I can offer a few more."

Then I recounted to him my thoughts about my 360° feedback. "You know me, Tom. Do you have any idea what my communication challenges might be? I'm certainly not the best communicator around, but I didn't think it was that big of an issue."

"Since I'm not in your department, it's difficult to know what the issue might be, but let me throw out a thought." Tom paused for a moment. "In my experience, information flow throughout the organization tends to bottleneck when it reaches the mid-level managers. These leaders tend to filter information and block the natural flow of communication up and down the organization. It's sort of like…" Tom seemed to be reaching for an analogy.

"…a blocked carotid artery, perhaps?" I offered.

"Interesting comparison," he said.

"Well, believe me, I've had lots of time to think about the problems that a blockage can cause. The more I think about it, the more I see that an organization is a lot like the human body. Let me show you what I mean. Will you hand me that pad and pen?"

I pulled the portable table across the bed, took the pad and pen, and drew an outline of a human body. "The brain is like senior management. It's the organ that makes decisions, sets the direction, coordinates, and gives instructions to the rest of the body."

Tom chuckled. "Does that mean IT is the 'left brain' and HR is the 'right brain'?"

"As a matter of fact, that's pretty much on target," I smiled. "But there are other parallels too. The neck, including all the veins and arteries, represents middle management. The neck connects the brain and the body, just as middle management is the connection between senior management and the rest of the organization. All the muscles of the body represent team members and associates – they carry out the movement or the work of the organization."

"That's a great analogy," Tom said enthusiastically. "I like it! Can I add some?"

"Sure," I answered, handing him the pen and paper.

"The heart represents the organization's values or culture," he said, starting to sketch. "The lungs are like sales and marketing –

they breathe life into the organization. A company can't survive without advertising, without getting its name and product offerings in front of the right customers. Bones symbolize the reporting structure of the organization. And, since we were talking about communication…it is represented by the blood. Blood carries oxygen, which corresponds to information – the lifeblood of the organization. So the circulatory system is like the organization's information system or communication flow."

"Hey, we're good!" I said, looking at our human body with its labeled parts and corresponding organizational functions.

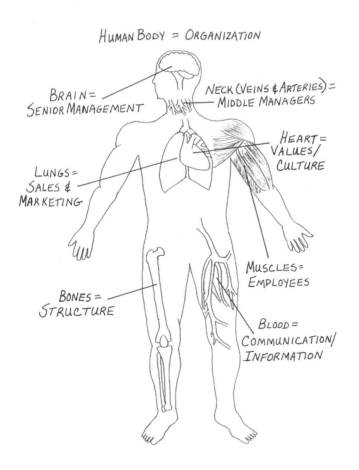

HUMAN BODY = ORGANIZATION

BRAIN = SENIOR MANAGEMENT

NECK (VEINS & ARTERIES) = MIDDLE MANAGERS

HEART = VALUES/ CULTURE

LUNGS = SALES & MARKETING

MUSCLES = EMPLOYEES

BONES = STRUCTURE

BLOOD = COMMUNICATION/ INFORMATION

"I've never thought about an organization like this before, but it makes perfect sense," said Tom with admiration. "Let's try the analogy with your question about communication and see if it works."

"Okay," I said. "Go for it."

"When the flow of oxygen-carrying blood is restricted throughout the body, you have big problems, right? You know about that firsthand. And when managers restrict the flow of information throughout the organization, it has big problems – at both the executive level and the team-member level. Let's say, for example, that a mid-level leader has a meeting with senior management, but he never debriefs with his team. When the leader is silent, the team starts to wonder what went on in that meeting."

"I have to admit I tend to do that," I said. "The team automatically assumes there's bad news, because otherwise the manager would have told them about the meeting."

"That's true," nodded Tom. "Then the rumor mill starts cranking – especially when a company is experiencing challenges like ours is now. In the absence of information, people start speculating – maybe senior management is planning layoffs, maybe the company or division is up for sale, maybe salary cuts are coming."

"I've seen what the rumor mill can do," I said. "You know, it's not that I don't want to tell my team what happened or that there are any big secrets. It's just that communicating what happened in some meeting doesn't seem that important compared to all the other things I have to do."

"I'm not saying team members need to know everything that goes on in management meetings," said Tom, "but I've seen how a complete lack of communication creates downstream problems. Leaders often think that keeping things quiet helps the team, but it actually hurts more than it helps. One tactic I tried was to give my team a quick, five-minute update after each meeting on the key things I learned. I realized there's always something you can tell the team – even if it's that you can't talk about the issues now, but you will as soon as you can. As leaders, communicating is one of the most important things we do."

"Sure, it's important," I said. "But it's hard to find time for it when we're busy putting out fires, making sure projects stay on schedule, following up with people to make sure they're doing what they're supposed to be doing, going to meetings, completing reports for senior management, answering a gazillion emails...you know how it is."

"I do know. Been there. But I also learned the hard way that nothing is more important than communicating with your team." He paused. "The good news is that once I made communicating effectively with my team one of my top priorities, about half of those things you mentioned – like putting out fires and keeping on top of employees and projects – simply went away."

He paused again. "Let me ask you a hypothetical question: If a leader doesn't have a structured way of communicating with his or her team, what are the consequences?"

I thought for a few seconds and then said, "Well, first of all, team members would probably be unclear about their priorities and objectives. That would lead to poor decision making about where to focus their time and attention, resulting in reduced productivity. And...I guess if the leader isn't communicating with them, it's more difficult for them to communicate effectively with the leader. So there's no feedback loop. They'd probably feel that they have no input or involvement in decisions. And they would feel disengaged and disconnected from the rest of the organization...morale would probably suffer."

"I think those are pretty safe assumptions. Any of those sound familiar to you?"

"Yes, unfortunately." I said. "You know, I hate it when you're right."

Tom pointed to the drawing on the table. "Here's something to think about. We said that the heart represents values or culture. What do your values and your department's culture say about communication? Do they reinforce that it's okay to communicate freely? Or do your unspoken values and your actions tell your team that really it's not okay to share information freely?"

"Well, I've always told my team they can come to me with anything – that my door is always open for them."

"That's good. But as the old saying goes, talk is cheap. It's your actions that are most important – that's what your team pays attention to. So the real question is, are your behaviors consistent with what you say to your team?"

It was another one of those zingers Tom threw out to make you stop and think. Just then a nurse came in to check my vitals. I was glad for the interruption. It gave me a chance to think about Tom's question. As the nurse took my pulse, blood pressure and temperature, I thought back over the last few months. I recalled a team meeting where one of my team leaders told me the customer satisfaction metrics weren't looking good and might hurt our quarterly bonus. With a wince, I remembered that I hadn't exactly received the news warmly. In fact, I told the team leader, somewhat loudly, not to bring me problems, but to bring me solutions instead. I'd told him, "Do what you have to do to get the numbers right."

Then I thought back to other meetings when I had glossed over problems that team members had wanted to discuss. And then there was that bad habit I had of ignoring phone calls and emails that involved problems.

After the nurse left the room, I answered Tom. "You know, in thinking about it, perhaps my actions don't always match my words. I tell employees it's okay to bring me their problems, but lately, the last thing I want to hear about is more problems. So I probably haven't reacted very well to people bringing me bad news."

Tom held up the piece of paper with the body sketch so I could see it. "If you don't keep your heart healthy, it can't properly pump blood throughout the body, and parts of the body, including the muscles, will start to deteriorate. Likewise, if your culture isn't healthy, information and communication won't flow throughout your department or the organization. As a result, parts of the organization won't function effectively."

"That's exactly what's happening in my department. Team members aren't working well together, we're not meeting project timelines, quality has suffered and productivity is down," I said.

I paused for a minute to think about the things we'd talked about. "I guess I'd better give some thought to other areas where what I do contradicts what I say."

■　■　■　■　■

About an hour later, an orderly showed up and took me back to reality – to the "cath lab." Time for more information gathering, I thought. Now we'd finally have the last piece of the puzzle.

After giving me a mild sedative, the doctor began the angiogram. In this relaxed state, my mind wandered back to the similarities Tom and I had talked about between organizations and the body. Thinking about my neck and how it corresponded to my role as a mid-level leader, the irony hit me. Here I was having an angiogram to examine my blockage, but *I* was the blockage in my organization. Tom and I had joked about the comparison, but now I realized how I'd hit the nail on the head without even knowing it. Just as plaque had blocked my carotid artery, stopping the flow of blood between my brain and my body, I had been blocking communication between senior management and my department.

Instead of listening to what my team members on the front lines were telling me and then passing all of that information on to senior management, I'd been selectively communicating – picking and choosing what to tell them and leaving some details out completely. As a result, the executive team had been making decisions based on faulty and incomplete information. Even worse, there were some issues they didn't even know about. I hadn't wanted to tell senior management the bad news: we needed new equipment in order to keep up with current production demands; many of our competitors had a faster turnaround than we did; and our key competitor had recently added the new features customers were asking for. Our competitors had a big head start on us that would be difficult to overcome.

Now I absolutely understood that the longer you ignore a problem – any problem – the bigger it gets.

■   ■   ■   ■   ■

When I returned to my room from the angiogram, I was surprised to see Tom was still there, waiting for me.

"So, what did you find out?" he asked with concern.

I groaned. "You know how we joked about the blockage in the carotid artery? Well, in our organization, I'm it!"

"What makes you say that?"

"I realized that because I haven't been communicating all the critical information with senior management, they couldn't make timely and informed decisions. Because the information flow was cut off, the organization's brain couldn't function properly."

Tom looked like he was about to say something, but I kept talking. Somehow everything I'd thought about made sense, and I needed to get all my thoughts out while I still remembered them.

"And you know how the analysts have been giving us negative reviews because the executive team hasn't been able to clearly explain the product recall to stockholders? That's also because of poor communication between the organization and the executive team. If internal information is filtered or watered down, external communication is impacted – just like what happened to me. When the blood going to my brain was temporarily cut off, my ability to communicate with the outside world was affected – I couldn't speak clearly and my speech was slurred."

As I shared these revelations with Tom, the knot in my stomach kept growing. "And because I haven't been communicating critical information back to my team – the muscles of the organization – they can't function properly either. When I was having the TIA, my arm and hand were weak and numb. The people on my team are like that, too. They're just going through the motions – they have no passion or enthusiasm. They're numb to external factors as well – to what customers are saying and to feedback from suppliers and other departments. And it's all because I've done a lousy job of communicating with them."

"And unfortunately, weakness in one department directly and negatively impacts other departments," said Tom.

"That's right," I nodded. "When one set of muscles doesn't work properly, other muscles have to compensate. If one team isn't functioning well, other departments have to pick up the slack and

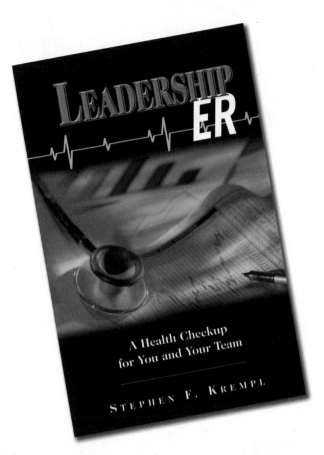

A Health Checkup
for You and Your Team

STEPHEN F. KREMPL

3 Easy Ways to Order
Copies for Your
Management Team!

1. Complete the order form on back and fax
   to 972-274-2884

2. Visit www.cornerstoneleadership.com

3. Call 1-888-789-LEAD (5323)

CornerStone
Leadership Institute

Passionate Performance: Engaging Minds and Hearts to Conquer the Competition is a quick read offering practical strategies to engage the minds and hearts of your team at home, work, church or community. Learn why this is such a powerful advantage for your organization. Read it and conquer your competition! **$9.95**

Sticking To It: The Art of Adherence reveals the secrets to success for high-achieving individuals and teams. It offers practical steps to help you consistently execute your plans. Read it and WIN! **$9.95**

Monday Morning Leadership is David Cottrell's newest and best-selling book. It offers unique encouragement and direction that will help you become a better manager, employee, and person. **$12.95**

NEW!

Monday Morning Leadership Audio CD $19.95

Management Insights explores the myths and realities of management. It provides insight into how you can become a successful manager. **$14.95**

Manager's Communication Handbook will allow you to connect with employees and create the understanding, support and acceptance critical to your success. **$9.95**

The Manager's Coaching Handbook is a practical guide to improve performance from your superstars, middle stars and falling stars. **$9.95**

175 Ways to Get More Done in Less Time has 175 really, really good suggestions that will help you get things done faster... and usually better. **$9.95**

Becoming the Obvious Choice is a roadmap showing each employee how they can maintain their motivation, develop their hidden talents, and become the best. **$9.95**

180 Ways to Walk the Recognition Talk is packed full with proven ideas and techniques that will help you provide recognition to your people more often and more effective. **$9.95**

Best Seller! Over 750,000 in Print

136 Effective Presentation Tips provides you with inside tips from two of the best presenters in the world. **$9.95**

Listen Up, Leader! Ever wonder what employees think about their leaders? This book tells you the seven characteristics of leadership that people will follow. **$9.95**

Leader's Performance Package
11 Dynamic Books + 1 Audio CD

$129.95

☑ **YES! Please send me extra copies of *Leadership ER!***

1-30 copies $14.95   31-100 copies $13.95   100+ copies $12.95

| Leadership ER | ___ copies X ___ | = $ ___ |

Additional Leadership Development Resources

Passionate Performance	___ copies X $9.95	= $ ___
Sticking to It: The Art of Adherence	___ copies X $9.95	= $ ___
Monday Morning Leadership	___ copies X $12.95	= $ ___
Monday Morning Leadership Audio CD	___ copies X $19.95	= $ ___
Management Insights	___ copies X $14.95	= $ ___
The Manager's Communication Handbook	___ copies X $9.95	= $ ___
The Manager's Coaching Handbook	___ copies X $9.95	= $ ___
175 Ways to Get More Done in Less Time	___ copies X $9.95	= $ ___
Becoming the Obvious Choice	___ copies X $9.95	= $ ___
180 Ways to Walk the Recognition Talk	___ copies X $9.95	= $ ___
136 Effective Presentation Tips	___ copies X $9.95	= $ ___
Listen Up, Leader!	___ copies X $9.95	= $ ___

Leader's Performance Package   ___ packs X $129.95   = $ ___
   (one of each of the items above,
   except Leadership ER)

	Shipping & Handling	$ ___
	Subtotal	$ ___
	Sales Tax (8.25%-TX Only)	$ ___
	Total (U.S. Dollars Only)	$ ___

Shipping and Handling Charges

Total $ Amount	Up to $49	$50-$99	$100-$249	$250-$1199	$1200-$2999	$3000+
Charge	$6	$9	$16	$30	$80	$125

Name _____ Job Title _____

Organization _____ Phone _____

Shipping Address _____ Fax _____

Billing Address _____ Email _____

City _____ State _____ Zip _____

❑ Please invoice (Orders over $200) Purchase Order Number (if applicable) _____

Charge Your Order: ❑ MasterCard   ❑ Visa   ❑ American Express

Credit Card Number _____ Exp. Date _____

Signature _____

❑ Check Enclosed (Payable to CornerStone Leadership)

Fax: 972.274.2884
Phone: 888.789.5323   www.**cornerstoneleadership**.com   **Mail: P.O. Box 764087**
                                                                           Dallas, TX 75376

carry the weight, and that creates inefficiencies."

"Mike, I think you're right to accept responsibility for your part in all this," Tom said. "But you make it sound as if you're solely responsible for all the problems our company is facing, and that's simply not the case. I think you're being too hard on yourself."

"I know I'm not solely responsible, but I'm clearly part of the problem," I said. "The worst part is that I'm probably not the only leader blocking the information flow. If I'm doing it, other leaders probably are too. What happens to the organization if sales, marketing or customer service aren't fully communicating with senior management and with other departments? I wonder how many bad decisions senior management has made because they didn't have all the information? It's no wonder we're having challenges!"

I paused for a minute. "And if *I'm* not communicating upward, what are the chances my team members aren't communicating *with me?*"

"Probably pretty good," Tom replied.

"More than likely, my team members filter the information they give me just like I do with those above me. So now *I* don't know the whole story and have probably made bad decisions because I didn't have all the information I needed."

Although the knot in the pit of my stomach had mushroomed into full-blown nausea, there was some relief in getting everything out in the open. I had been thinking my team members were responsible for the problems in our department. But the truth was that *I* was the biggest problem. Sure, my employees played a role, but ultimately, it all came down to me. I was the leader.

Tom seemed to sense what I was feeling. "If it's any consolation, Mike, this is the toughest part. Things can't get better until you fully understand the scope of the problem and accept responsibility.

Then you can formulate a plan and do something about it."

"I know. You're right," I said. "I didn't expect to diagnose my work problems until I got back, but it's starting to look like communication is the issue. My lack of communication has hurt not only my department, but also the entire organization."

I sat back and sighed. "At least now I know what's wrong – with my health and with my department. Now I've got to determine the best treatment plan."

A TIME TO REFLECT

The Comfort of Knowing

Mike realized that his diagnosis might not be good news. However, regardless of whether the news was good or bad, he could only take appropriate action once he knew what the problem was. Answer these questions to move toward positive action in your life.

Personal Health

♦ Do you have a thorough understanding of your current health status?

♦ What problems do you have that need a defined treatment regimen?

♦ Are you ready to accept complete responsibility for your own health? If not, why?

♦ What would it take to get you to accept that responsibility?

Business Health

♦ Do you have a thorough understanding of your current business problems?

♦ How do you ensure you will get to the root cause of your problems before diving in to find a solution?

♦ What is currently distracting you from identifying the problems?

♦ Are you ready to accept complete responsibility for your team's health? If not, why?

♦ What would it take to get you to accept responsibility?

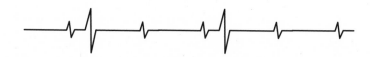

5

THE POWER
OF CHOOSING

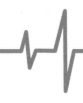

> *"There are two primary choices in life: to accept conditions as they exist, or accept the responsibility for changing them."*
>
> – Dennis Waitley

Lynda and I were making small talk when Dr. Lee returned. I found myself holding my breath. Finally I'd be able to start taking action.

"I have good news," she said. "The angiogram revealed only a 40 percent blockage in your carotid artery. With that amount of blockage, I generally do not recommend surgery. I think your best bet would be to make some changes to your lifestyle. You should be okay if you can stick to a good diet, exercise regularly, and faithfully take the medications I'll prescribe for you."

I let out my breath in a long sigh of relief. Lynda smiled at me and squeezed my hand, and I could see the relief on her face. I turned to the doctor. "Lynda has promised to be my watchdog and make me take my medications. And I'll do my best to stay on an exercise program and a healthy diet."

"Mike," said Dr. Lee, sighing, "I hope you realize that making these changes isn't an option for you at this point. I don't like the sound of 'I'll do my best.' You *must* make significant changes and you *must* keep taking the medications. If you don't, you will almost certainly have another TIA or even worse, a stroke. More than likely, a stroke would cause some kind of permanent damage."

"Mike, you absolutely have to stick to the plan," said Lynda. "No giving up in week two like last time." Her face was set and serious too. Then she turned to Dr. Lee and said, "I'll make sure he follows the regimen this time."

"I appreciate that, Lynda, but you can't be with him 24 hours a day. Mike, you're very fortunate to have a loving wife who is supportive and cares about you a great deal. Perhaps your children will also want to get involved and support you. But in the end, it all comes down to you." Her voice took on a steely tone, and I knew she was dead serious. "You have to accept responsibility for your health. You must commit to doing what it takes to get healthy and stay healthy. It's not going to be easy, but it will be for the best."

"I know it won't be easy…" I said. Man, was that an understatement! I wasn't lazy – it's just that life was busy and stressful enough already. I didn't want to have to think about everything I ate. I didn't need more pressure. At my age, it was going to be hard to change my couch-potato lifestyle and cholesterol-packed diet. But then I had a vision of myself collapsed on the floor and it scared me. "…but of course I'll do it. I don't have any choice."

"Good," said Dr. Lee. "Now, let's talk more about the specific changes you need to make." She scrawled something on her prescription pad and handed it to me. "This is a prescription, Mike. But this one isn't for medication. These are the five changes I'm prescribing for you."

I took the paper. On it she had written just five words: MEDICATION, EXERCISE, DIET, RELAX and CHECKUPS.

"Let me explain to you what each of those means," she said.

"First, take the medication I prescribe – faithfully. Follow all the directions and don't skip any days. You'll have two medications: one to reduce your blood pressure, and another to thin your blood to prevent blood clots from forming or breaking off and causing a stroke."

"We'll get you one of those weekly pill minders," said Lynda.

"Second, you need to exercise – enough to raise your heart rate – at least 20 minutes, three times a week."

"I guess that means riding in the golf cart is out," I said dryly.

"Third," Dr. Lee continued, without missing a beat, "you need to lower your cholesterol and lose about 30 pounds. I don't want any fad diets here. You need to eat a well-balanced diet with less sugar, fewer bad fats and more fruits, vegetables, and good fats. Do you know the difference between good and bad fats?"

"Well, sort of," hedged Lynda. "You mean eat more olive oil, right?"

"I'll ask a nutritionist to stop by and talk to you. Number four, relax! Try to reduce the stress in your life. You seem to be carrying a tremendous load of stress, Mike. Am I right?"

I nodded. "A tremendous load" didn't begin to cover these last few months.

"High-stress work environments can be an enemy if they're not handled well," said Dr. Lee. "Many people find that exercise is a good way to reduce stress. And finally, come in for checkups every six months. I want to keep tabs on your progress."

"You're not asking for much are you, doc?" I said. "To do all this will take a major overhaul of my life!"

"Many of my patients who've had trouble making these kinds of changes do better when they partner with some experts," she said. "These people are excellent sources of information and support. I recommend you find an internist that you like and trust – one you can work with to develop a long-term plan to continually improve your health. Some patients find it worthwhile to invest in a few sessions with a personal trainer to help them structure an exercise program they will enjoy and therefore will be more likely to stick with. And, as I mentioned earlier, we have an excellent nutritionist here at the hospital who can help you two understand how to choose and prepare healthier foods. Please don't try to travel this road alone."

"Those are some good suggestions. There's a gym just down the street from our house – I'll see about getting a trainer to help me out."

"Well, I think that's about it," the doctor said. "Are you still feeling okay?"

"Much better. Especially now that I've made a choice about a treatment plan."

"If you promise to stay home and take it easy for a few days, I don't see any reason why you can't go home this afternoon."

Great news! I couldn't wait to see the kids. "Thank you, Doctor, for everything."

"Yes," Lynda added, "thank you. And could you please arrange for the nutritionist to come by this afternoon before we leave? I want to start making some changes as soon as we get home."

After Dr. Lee left, Lynda and I embraced each other tightly. The crisis was over.

Eventually, Lynda released her hug and stepped back. There were tears in her eyes. As she dabbed at her eyes with a tissue, she said, "Sweetheart, I'm going to run down and get something to eat. I'll be back in a little bit, okay?"

"Okay, honey. Take your time. I'll be fine here."

Lynda smiled. "Good. You know, I could barely sleep last night at the thought of you..."

"Don't say it," I said as I touched her lips. "I'm not going anywhere."

After she left, I sat for a moment, trying to digest everything the doctor had said. Then I picked up the phone and called Tom.

"So how do you feel about making such major changes?" he asked when I'd told him about the results of the angiogram and the doctor's prescription. "I know I'd have trouble following all five parts of the prescription."

"It's funny. Even though I know it will be hard, I feel strangely empowered…at least about my health. I guess I need to make some choices about work, too. But that won't be easy either."

"Making big changes is seldom easy, but it's usually worth the effort."

"It just seems like there are so many changes I need to make with my team – I'm not sure where to start."

"What if you followed the same prescription for your team that the doctor gave you for your health? You could start with all those parallels you found between the ER and your problems at work, and then connect the actions you need to take to improve your health with the actions you need to take to improve the health of your department. Perhaps that would help you focus your energies and improve your chances of success."

"That's an interesting thought," I said. "And it's the obvious way to start. I saw so many parallels between the two areas of my life. Maybe I'll come up with five strategies for restoring health to my department – something along the lines of what the doctor gave me."

"Great idea, Mike. You can approach it with the same kind of methodology. You'll probably want to think about changes to your leadership practices, your department's culture, and your processes and procedures."

"You've just given me an idea on how to begin." I was becoming more intrigued as I started to imagine different pieces of the plan.

"There's one obvious connection. The doctor said I need to exercise regularly to strengthen my cardiovascular system. The business correlation could be that I need to get some leadership training to strengthen my communication skills."

"Actually it could be even broader than just training," added Tom. "The correlation could be anything you do to strengthen skills and gain knowledge, including reading books, attending seminars, benchmarking, doing research or talking to a good communicator."

"You're right. I'll work on that idea. Thanks for the suggestion."

■　■　■　■　■

After talking to Tom, I felt energized, and I couldn't wait to begin working on my plan. I took out the laptop I had begged Lynda to bring and started to capture my thoughts. First, I created a chart to record the connections between my personal health strategies and my business health strategies. Underneath the heading PERSONAL Rx, I typed the five words Dr. Lee had given me: MEDICATION, EXERCISE, DIET, RELAX and CHECKUPS.

Beside EXERCISE and in the column titled BUSINESS Rx, I typed what Tom and I had talked about: "Strengthen communication skills." There. One down, four to go.

MEDICATION was first on the list, so I went back to it. Now what was the parallel in business for taking medications? For some reason, I kept coming back to a climate survey HR had recently conducted. I remembered getting the results for my department, but not really knowing what to make of them. One thing did come through loud and clear – morale was at an all-time low. I made a note to review the survey results again as soon as I got back in the office and dig deeper to find the cause behind the morale problem.

Once I accurately diagnosed the problem, I'd remedy the situation as soon as possible.

Ha! That was it! I smiled to myself. "Remedy" – like medicine! The remedy I'd use to improve employee morale would correlate to the new medicines I'd be taking to lower my blood pressure and thin my blood. Beside MEDICATION I added: "TO DO: Find remedy to improve employee morale."

Personal R_x	Business R_x
Medication	TO DO: Find remedy to improve employee morale
Exercise	Strengthen communication skills

The next word on the list was DIET. How could there possibly be a business parallel for that? I decided to skip that one and come back to it later. I left the space next to the word DIET blank.

RELAX was next. This health crisis had convinced me I was missing out on my children's lives, and I definitely missed spending time with my wife. So when Dr. Lee said I needed to relax more and reduce my stress level, I knew immediately I'd do that by spending more quality time with my family. I wanted to rebuild my relationships with my wife and kids – get to know them again.

Relax…reduce stress…rebuild relationships. Was there a business connection there?

Certainly stress was a major factor at work and had a profound effect on my relationship with my team. It was the main reason I was impatient with team members and didn't take time to communicate with them. Stress was like the plaque that filled my arteries, and it blocked the communication flow between us. In fact, the stress was so intense in our department, it had destroyed the trust my team members had in me.

Stress was also the reason I filtered the information I gave senior management. With all the challenges the organization was facing, senior management was under a lot of pressure. I sure didn't want to be the proverbial straw that broke the camel's back by giving them even more bad news. The truth was, I had been concerned about losing my job for a while, which of course added to my stress level considerably. I was afraid that if I shared all the ugly details with senior management, they might decide I couldn't handle the job. It all came down to the issue of trust again. I needed to trust that the leaders on the senior management team weren't out to get me and that they didn't expect me to be perfect. And of course, those same leaders needed to trust that I would be honest with them and not withhold critical information.

It was becoming obvious that trust was the foundation of good communication. If things were going to get better, I'd have to rebuild trust – both downward with my team and upward with the executives. And to build trust and reduce our team's stress, I'd have to rebuild relationships. Sure, it would take some time, but it was an investment of time and energy that would pay off.

Reduce stress…build relationships…build trust. It wasn't exactly a parallel, but it was a connection. And that was good enough for me. I added the words "reduce stress" after the word RELAX in the chart and then typed "Build relationships…build trust" next to that.

The fifth strategy prescribed for me was CHECKUPS. Seeing a doctor regularly would keep me accountable and ensure that I was on track with the changes I needed to make. But the checkups would also give me the chance to measure my progress: How much weight had I lost? How much had I lowered my blood pressure?

I could create a similar situation at work. I'd find someone to be accountable to, someone who would hold my feet to the fire. Maybe that was Tom...or maybe Carmen. We'd meet regularly to make sure I was on track. And just as my doctor would take my blood pressure, run a blood test to check my cholesterol or do a follow-up ultrasound to measure the blockage in my artery, I would check for measurable improvement in my department by conducting follow-up climate surveys, customer satisfaction surveys, and team-based profiles. The result would be an ongoing plan for the continuous improvement of my department's health. Beside the word CHECKUPS I added "Be accountable and measure progress."

Personal R$_x$	Business R$_x$
Medication	TO DO: Find remedy to improve employee morale
Exercise	Strengthen communication skills
Diet	
Relax/reduce stress	Build relationships...build trust
Checkups	Be accountable and measure progress

I looked at the chart and was pleased with what I'd accomplished – it was a good start. I still had to find a connection for DIET, but I needed to think about that one for a while to find a good business parallel.

But now it was time to take care of another important task. Something had been nagging at me since my panic attack yesterday. When I thought for certain it was the end, I felt tremendous sadness and guilt for my obsession with work. When it came right down to it, how important was work, really? If I had died, would I have wanted people to remember me for how many hours I'd spent at the office or for my commitment to my family? It didn't take much thought to answer that one. I decided to take some time off and spend it with my family.

Lynda had been saying for years that she wanted to take a trip to San Francisco and the Napa Valley. I searched the Internet and found a travel website. Within minutes I had booked airline tickets and hotel reservations for a long-deserved vacation for Lynda and me. I needed some time with Josh and Rachel, too, and I committed to make that time. But first and foremost, Lynda and I needed some time together.

Lynda returned to the room just as I was finishing up and caught me on the laptop. I closed it quickly, like a child caught sneaking candy. She shook her head in amazement. "I can't believe you're working from your hospital bed. I can only hope that part of your prescription is a vacation."

I smiled a knowing smile.

■　■　■　■　■

Later that afternoon, the nutritionist came up and spent some time teaching Lynda and me about healthy eating. I realized that for years I'd been eating too much fat, sugar and salt. No wonder my body had rebelled. Toward the end of the meeting, Lynda paraphrased what the nutritionist had said: "So what you're saying, in a nutshell, is that Mike needs to eat more healthy foods – like fruits, vegetables, lean proteins and complex carbohydrates – and less junk food, fast food, and sweets. Is that right?" It was obvious she was saying it more for me to hear than to confirm the nutritionist's instructions.

I laughed. "I hear you. I need to say yes to the good stuff and no to the bad stuff." The nutritionist, obviously annoyed, said I was oversimplifying things, but she did agree that was more or less the point.

That phrase I'd used about saying yes to the good stuff and no to the bad kept echoing in my head. Where had I heard that before? And then it came to me. Tom had used that phrase in a conversation we'd had about six weeks ago.

"We're suffering from information and activity overload," he'd said. "We have to say yes to the meaningful information and say no to the extraneous information that distracts from the message. Likewise, we need to say yes to activities and tasks that support the team's purpose and say no to those that distract from the purpose."

We'd been talking about how we – meaning both leaders and employees – receive so much information and have so many things to do that it's difficult to sort out what's important to our jobs and what's not.

"With so many communication methods available now – email, intranet, cell phones, PDAs, newsletters, memos – I think we spend more time thinking about *how* we're going to communicate than *what* we're going to communicate," I'd said. "We tend to focus more on responding than communicating effectively."

Tom had agreed.

"So what's the solution?" I'd thrown the question out for either of us to answer.

Tom jumped in. "Generally speaking, we don't need more information, we need higher quality information. That would allow us to better focus on the right kind of activities. We need to think of communication as an outcome, not as another activity. To do that, we have to look at communication from the receiver's perspective."

At the time, I thought it was a good answer, but now it made even more sense. Each person we communicate with has different information needs. Once we understand those needs, we can include more of the relevant information and cut out the irrelevant, just like Tom had said. Then it hit me – this was the parallel for DIET. We needed to put our overstuffed information on a diet to get rid of the excess. If everyone on the team chose wisely with respect to what information to communicate, we could all consume smaller portions.

But too much information was only half of the problem. We needed to slim down our burgeoning task lists also. We had to take a fresh look at the activities on our plates, and say yes to the important activities and say no to the urgent but unimportant ones. If we could do that, our productivity would go through the roof.

It was all kind of corny, but I liked the connection.

"Mike! Mike! Why are you smiling? Are you listening to what the nutritionist is saying?" Lynda whispered.

"Absolutely!" I lied. I made a mental note to add the final entry to my chart. Beside DIET I would add "Go on an information and activity diet." Then I turned my attention back to the nutritionist.

■　■　■　■　■

Finally it was time to go home. As the orderly pushed me down the hallway in the wheelchair, I realized how much I had changed in the two days I'd spent there. Curiously, the fear was gone, and I felt only a deep and sincere appreciation for the entire experience. I'd found out the hard way that my choices have real, and sometimes dire, consequences. Thankfully, I'd been given a second chance to make things right – to make changes so that I could survive. Now it was up to me to make the most of that chance. There was a transformative power in making a choice. I knew what I had to do – for my health and for my career. I had to take action.

A TIME TO REFLECT

The Power of Choosing

Mike had an important choice to make. He realized the value of partnering with a professional to help him make that life-changing commitment to improve his health. And, just as importantly, he sought help from Tom for his team issues. In both cases, he had to commit to take action in order to accomplish his goals. Answer these questions to help you identify important new actions that need to be taken in your life.

Personal Health

♦ Have you had a wake-up call with respect to your health? What did you learn from it?

♦ Do you have a primary physician or other health care professional willing to partner with you and assist you in developing an overall health plan?

♦ Have you identified changes you need to make in order to improve your health? Are you willing to work on those and make the necessary changes?

♦ Is there anything else you can do to improve your condition?

Business Health

♦ Have you had a wake-up call with respect to your team or department? What did you learn from it?

♦ Have you identified a partner to help you assess and improve the overall health of your team?

♦ Are you willing to take difficult action in order to improve the long-term health of your team?

♦ What recommendations have your customers, employees, colleagues or consultants made that you never implemented but should have?

♦ What else can you do to improve your team's performance?

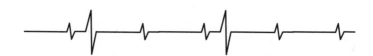

6 THE CHALLENGES OF TAKING ACTION

> *"A real decision is measured by the fact that you've taken a new action. If there's no action, you haven't truly decided."*
>
> – Anthony Robbins

After being released from the hospital, I took a few days off work. I took it easy – watched movies and played games with the kids and even helped them with their homework. After those few days at home, I made the commitment that we would go on a family vacation at least once a year.

Lynda and I agreed it would be best for me to be accountable to our children, Josh and Rachel, for my personal health plan. Being accountable to her could have led to trouble – it'd be too easy to feel like she was nagging me. The kids thought it was great fun to check up on me. And when my 7-year-old daughter looked up at me and asked, "Daddy, have you taken your medicine today?" or my son said, "Hey, Dad, let's go for a bike ride," well…it got to me. It was a constant reminder of the best reasons to get healthy and stay healthy.

Although I was still afraid that I'd be fired when I went back to work, I decided I couldn't dwell on that possibility. I had to think positively and start taking proactive steps to fix the problems in my department. So I took some time during those days off to develop and refine the specific changes I needed to make to restore health to my department.

In the hospital, I had decided that the correlation for my personal health strategy of MEDICATION would be a remedy for improving employee morale. So I called Denise, our HR director, and asked her to help me interpret my department's results from the climate survey. After some discussion about the results and the dynamics on my team, we reached a conclusion together: My team members were disengaged – they felt disconnected from their work, from each other and from the rest of the organization.

"When employees are disengaged, you've got problems," Denise explained. "Missed deadlines. A decline in productivity. Lack of accountability. Are you experiencing any of those symptoms in your department?"

"Yeah," I winced. "All of them."

"Recent studies have shown that communication is the number one factor in engaging employees," she continued. "In my experience, leaders always think they communicate better than they actually do. My advice is to work on improving the quality of your communication with your team."

I thanked her and hung up the phone. Communication. There it was again. It seemed to be at the root of all my department's problems. As I sat there thinking about ways I could improve my communication, I glanced over at my two new prescriptions – small pink pills and even smaller white pills. Then I smiled. I had it – the parallel for MEDICATION. I would create an acronym for the word *pill*.

The letter "P" – *Perspective*. That one came quickly. I remembered what Tom had said about looking at communication from each receiver's *unique perspective*. I would ask my team members what information they needed from me, why and when they needed it, and how I could best communicate it to them. Then I would ask Carmen the same questions. Knowing what information was meaningful to each receiver would dramatically improve the quality of my communication.

Then I thought about how people on my team were always saying, "I never heard that" or "No one told me about...." Apparently I wasn't including all the appropriate people in my communications. That was it. The letter "I" would stand for *Include everyone*. Before I sent out any communication, I would ask myself two questions: "Who is my target audience?" and "Have I included everyone that needs to know about this information?"

"L" was next. The word for that came quickly too – *logical Language*. How many times as an employee had I received rambling emails, voice mails and memos that jumped from one subject to another, with no clear point or message? Too many to count. Communication should contain only essential pieces of information and those should follow a logical sequence. I committed to check each message before it went out to be certain it was clear, to the point, and included language the target audience would understand – no unfamiliar jargon or acronyms.

If I were a team member, what else would I want in communication from my leaders? To understand how information relates to what I do every day. As a team member, I used to get bombarded with information, and most of the time it wasn't clear what I was to do with than information. Now, as a leader communicating with my team, I had to make the *Link obvious*. That was the word for the final "L." In all communication, it should be clear to the receivers how the information affects them – what the connection is between the information and their job or daily activities. Communication has failed if the receiver doesn't see the link between himself and the information.

PILL was the remedy. I went back to the chart I had started at the hospital. Next to MEDICATION, I added: "Take a communication PILL daily" and the words for each letter of the acronym.

Personal R_x	Business R_x
Medication	Take a communication PILL daily: Perspective Include Language Link
Exercise	Strengthen communication skills
Diet	Go on an information and activity diet
Relax/reduce stress	Build relationships...build trust
Checkups	Be accountable and measure progress

I reviewed the completed chart. Of course, the parallels between the personal and business strategies weren't perfect – and some were quite a stretch! But each of the five pairs was linked in some way in my mind, and those connections made it easier for me to focus on the changes I needed to make.

If I could make these changes happen, I knew the outcome would be positive. On the personal side, my blood pressure and cholesterol would improve, reducing my risk of a stroke. On the business side, the increased flow of communication throughout the organization meant senior management would get the information it needed to make informed and timely decisions, and my team would get the information it needed to complete its work and function smoothly.

■　　■　　■　　■　　■

My first day back at work came and went without incident, and I began to wonder if I had blown the whole situation out of proportion. But on the second day, Carmen emailed me from the road to reschedule our meeting to talk about "the problems in my department." Because of her travel schedule, it would be some time before we could meet. Apparently, I still had a job...at least for a while.

Over the following weeks, I made a dedicated effort to take action on the choices I had made. Both the neurologist and Tom had warned me it wouldn't be easy, and they were right! The choices that had seemed so obvious at the hospital were actually quite difficult to put into practice on a daily basis. Once the crisis was over and the urgency was gone, the motivation to change diminished.

Probably the hardest personal change was overcoming my long-standing couch-potato ways and exercising consistently. I quickly discovered that exercising at home didn't work, so I joined a gym and enlisted the help of a personal trainer. The first two weeks, I was motivated and worked out about four times each week. But before long, other things gradually began to encroach on my time at the gym – late afternoon business meetings, Josh's baseball games, Rachel's soccer games. It seemed there was always something more urgent than exercising.

Meanwhile, Lynda was doing a lot of reading about healthy eating. Suddenly every food that tasted good disappeared from the refrigerator and pantry – apparently eating healthy is an acquired taste. I tried to make better choices at lunchtime, but most days I simply didn't have time to go to a restaurant for a healthy meal, so I resorted to fast food more than I should have.

Even taking my pills consistently was a challenge. Really the only front on which I was making consistent progress was my commitment to relax more (even though I was still fairly stressed about all the challenges at work). We started a family game night with the kids, and Lynda and I had a weekly date night.

Just as I was trying to make changes in my personal life, I was also working hard to improve the condition of my department – with mixed results. I invested in some communication skills training and walked away with six action items I wanted to implement back on the job. I applied my new skills religiously for a couple of weeks, but when I didn't see tangible results as quickly as I wanted, the changes fell by the wayside.

I discovered it was much easier to remember to take my communication PILL than my blood pressure pill. That acronym was so vivid it stuck in my mind, and every time I got ready to send out a message, I'd think about those four key characteristics. I knew it was making a difference when I started getting positive feedback about my memos and emails.

Unfortunately, it wasn't so easy to stick to my activity diet. There were too many temptations. I had good intentions, but when I got back into the daily grind, it was just too easy to get distracted by urgent activities and lose sight of what was important. Before I knew it, I was back to my old habits and my task list was bigger than ever.

I did try especially hard to regain my team's trust. After I got back to work, I called a meeting with my employees and apologized and accepted responsibility for the communication problems we'd had. Although they appeared to believe me, I knew it would be a long time before they really felt comfortable approaching me with a problem. Regaining their trust wouldn't happen quickly or easily.

I had more success rebuilding my relationship with Carmen. I initiated biweekly meetings with her to review my projects and discuss what was going on in my department. These meetings really improved my communication up the organization to senior management. Instead of filtering information, I told Carmen exactly how I saw things. Sometimes I even brought in a team member to talk with her directly to eliminate any "spin" I might put on the information.

Overall, I was making progress, but neither I nor my department was the rosy picture of health I had envisioned five weeks ago when I left the hospital. Taking action wasn't as easy as I had thought it would be.

Carmen and I did finally have our meeting about the problems in my department. This was the meeting that had started it all – the one that had kept me up all night worrying about being fired. I went in armed with my chart that outlined the changes I was implementing. I reviewed each strategy in detail with her and shared the progress I was making on each one. When I finished, she smiled a big smile – uncharacteristic for Carmen – and said she could tell the situation was improving.

And that was it. She didn't fire me. She didn't even put me on notice. But I couldn't shake the feeling that there had been more planned for the original meeting than Carmen let on.

■　　■　　■　　■　　■

One morning a few weeks later, Tom and I met for coffee before work. It was the first time we'd gotten together since I'd been in the hospital.

"So how's everything going?" he asked.

For the next five minutes, I unloaded on him. I talked about the good things that were happening, but mostly I talked about all my frustrations and disappointments. "I know I have to make these changes in my life and at work," I said when I'd finished, "and I want to change, but it just isn't happening."

"Relax, Mike. Don't be so hard on yourself. I think you've bitten off more than you can chew – you're trying to make too many changes at once."

"You're right," I said gloomily. "I'm completely overwhelmed."

"It's hard to break old habits. You've had these habits and this comfortable routine for years. You can't expect to change all of that overnight. You didn't get in this situation in one day, and you're not going to get out of it in a day either. It's going to take consistent effort over weeks, months, maybe even years in some cases."

I groaned. "I know. I need to have more reasonable expectations. I just wish there was some way to speed things up. I need some success to give me the momentum to keep going."

Tom looked thoughtful for a moment. "What if you tried breaking it down? When things seem overwhelming to me, I break them down into smaller, more manageable chunks and then focus on just one piece at a time."

"But the neurologist said I have to make progress in all five areas. There's no way I can go back to her and say I've done only one thing."

"I'm hardly qualified to give advice on eating right or exercising because I struggle with those issues as well," Tom said. "I can only tell you that in trying to change my own habits, I've read that when you need to make several changes, it's best to pick one and focus on it. They say it takes 30 days to create a new positive habit. So pick the one change, or action item, that will have the biggest impact and focus on it until you can do it well and it becomes a habit. Then choose the action that will have the next biggest impact and make it a habit. Keep doing that until you establish a whole new set of positive habits that will lead to better health."

"But how am I supposed to pick?" I said in exasperation. "What am I supposed to do — not take my medications?" Immediately I regretted my comment, but Tom seemed to let it slide by.

"Doing five things poorly or inconsistently isn't going to have much affect on your health," he said calmly. "Clearly, the medications are the most critical aspect of your personal health changes. If I were you, I'd concentrate first on taking your medications. Don't worry about exercising or the diet. If you find time to exercise or you eat well during that time, great – it's a bonus.

"Over the next 30 days, do whatever you have to so that you remember to take your pills. Maybe you can set the alarm on your watch so that no matter where you are, you'll be reminded to take them. Or maybe you need to put them in your pocket so you'll have them with you all the time. Initially, you might want to have Lynda remind you, but ultimately you're responsible for taking the medication. So find out how to make it work best for *you*."

"I know I'll need some sort of alarm or physical reminder," I said.

"Then set an alarm every single day for 30 days. If you do, I'll bet that taking your medications when you're supposed to, day in and day out, won't be a problem any more. You will have created a new habit – one that fits your lifestyle and that will work for you for the rest of your life."

"You're right. I need to try harder to find what suits my style." I sipped my coffee and thought for a moment. "After I establish a routine with my medications, I guess I should ask my doctor what part of the prescription I should focus on next."

Tom nodded. "I think that's a good idea. She'd be able to tell you which piece of the plan will have the next biggest impact on your health – changing your diet or exercising."

"I don't know which is the lesser of two evils," I added. "But I'll do whatever I need to do until I've changed my habits."

"The key is to find a way that works for you," said Tom. "I've had trouble getting enough exercise myself, so I'm still trying to find what works for me. Someone suggested incorporating exercise into family activities, like taking the kids to the pool or to the park, so I might try that tactic next."

"Those are some good ideas." I stopped to take another sip of coffee. "I'm guessing you'll suggest I try the same approach at work – choose one action to focus on and make it a habit."

"I'm that predictable, huh?" he smiled. "Yeah, I'd suggest you pick the one strategy you think will have the greatest positive impact on the problems your team is facing. Figure out how to best make the strategy work given your team dynamics. Don't try to copy the way another leader or department does it. Sure, you can look to others for benchmarking ideas, but they're just that – ideas. Make it work for you and your team. Then commit to repeating the behavior or action every day until it becomes a habit."

"It's a great idea for implementing my plan at work too. It seems doable. I can see myself being successful if I approach it this way. I continue to be amazed at the ways our personal and professional lives so often parallel one another," I said thoughtfully. I paused to finish off the last of my coffee. "I have a favor to ask, Tom."

"Sure. Shoot."

"Well, with my personal changes, it's been a great help to have someone to be accountable to. At home, it's my kids. They do a great job of helping me stay on track. Would you be willing to help me with that at work?"

"Of course, Mike. I'd be happy to help you any way I can."

"Thanks. I appreciate it. I never dreamed it would be so hard to make these changes," I said, shaking my head. "You know, taking action on something doesn't seem like a big deal – until you actually have to do it. I *know* it's important to exercise, eat right, and build trust with my team. And I can *tell you* that I know it's important to do those things. But until I take action, I'm not *living* like it's important."

A TIME TO REFLECT

The Challenges of Taking Action

Mike discovered that it's one thing to talk about taking action; it's quite another to actually do it. He learned it's easy to get distracted and become overwhelmed when we try to make big changes in our lives. And, he found out that there was a process and a support system that could help him achieve success. Answer these questions to improve your chances of success.

Personal Health

♦ Do you have a plan for attaining and maintaining long-term health?

♦ Which aspect of your health plan could have the greatest positive impact on your health?

♦ How will you ensure you execute the plan systematically?

♦ Have you identified potential obstacles that could prevent you from executing your plan?

♦ What resources and support do you need to help you execute your health plan? Do you have access to those resources and support?

♦ Are you accountable to anyone other than yourself for implementing your health plan?

♦ How will you reward yourself for meeting your milestones?

Business Health

♦ Do you have a systematic plan (rather than temporary fixes) for attaining and maintaining the long-term health of your team?

♦ Which part of your plan, when implemented, could have the greatest positive impact on your team?

♦ What organization-wide resources could you utilize to support the change?

♦ What systems do you have to ensure team accountability?

♦ What historical obstacles get in the way of timely action? How will you remove or overcome these obstacles?

♦ How will you celebrate your team's success?

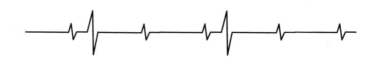

7

THE REWARDS
OF GOOD HEALTH

> "Our health always seems much more
> valuable after we lose it."
> – Author Unknown

Six months after my trip to the ER, I could finally say that things were back on track for me both personally and professionally. Tom's idea of focusing on one thing until it becomes a habit was a winner. I used it with my health plan and my plan at work. And before long I was seeing results.

I had established a good habit of taking both my medications every day. I was focused on improving my diet and was actually starting to enjoy some of the new foods I was saying yes to. I expected it would take longer than 30 days to establish healthy eating habits, but I was making great progress. Exercise was next on the priority list.

Lynda and I had been on a spectacular trip to northern California – the one I had booked while in the hospital. We decided to make it an annual getaway – just the two of us.

My six-month checkup with my new internist went better than I expected. I had lost 11 pounds, my cholesterol was down from 220 to 150, and my blood pressure had improved significantly. The doctor said I was off to a good start and that I would see more results if I continued the regimen. He also told me that, according to the statistics, most strokes happen within one year after a TIA. I was halfway home...so far, so good. Best of all, I felt better – more energetic and alive.

On the business side, my department had made a significant turnaround. Our projects were on schedule, productivity was up, and customer complaints were down. Of the five strategies I had developed to improve my team's health, my top priority was to build trust. Although I didn't think it would have the greatest short-term impact, I felt it was the foundation for the other strategies. Team members had started bringing problems to me again and were working together to resolve issues early. I quickly realized that building relationships and trust was not a habit that could be established in 30 days – it is a never-ending process.

I was working hard on my information diet to reduce the amount of information we consumed in our department. It was a challenging process because not only did I have to create a habit for myself, but I also had to help each team member create a habit. Improving the quality of the information I sent out was only half the battle. Everyone on the team had to reduce their communication.

We were also making good progress on our activity diet. My team liked the diet analogy, and we had a lot of fun with it. When we caught another team member doing something unnecessary or unimportant, we would jokingly scold that person for "cheating" on the diet.

I had successfully implemented one idea I'd gotten from the communication skills training and planned to start implementing another one in the coming months.

As with the changes in my personal life, I had found that 30 days to make a habit was the minimum. Although we could see some results after about 30 days, my team and I generally felt it took longer for the changes to become a way of life. It was one of those situations where you've got to slow down to speed up.

Communication with Carmen had continued to improve. At my first quarterly "checkup" with her, she shared her enthusiasm for the changes I had made in my department. Then she revealed that the original intent of that Friday afternoon meeting was to give me notice that my job was in jeopardy. But after my experience in the ER, she said she had sensed a change in me and had decided to wait a few months to see what would happen. She was impressed with my initiative and the performance improvement plan I had developed, and said it was clear it had made a positive impact on my leadership abilities. There was still more work to be done, but I was on the right track.

So, I had been right – my job had been in jeopardy. It was an odd feeling to know that I had been on the verge of two major crises in my life. Why did I get a second chance – especially when so many other people don't? Was it sheer luck? Was it chance? It certainly wasn't because of anything I had done. But one thing was for certain – I was grateful for the wake-up call and I was determined to take it seriously.

■　■　■　■　■

One day not too long ago, Tom and I had lunch together. He commented that I looked good. I told him I felt great, I'd had a positive checkup with my internist, and I was happy both personally and professionally. Life seemed to be back on track.

"So, Mike, it's been over six months since your trip to the ER. Have you taken the time to reflect on what you've learned from all of this?" It was a typical Tom philosophical question.

I knew him too well, and I was ready for the question. "I knew that question was coming sooner or later, Tom," I smiled. "I've been thinking about it for a few weeks. So here goes:

"First, don't ignore warning signs. Just because you feel okay doesn't mean you're healthy. Pay attention to recurring symptoms. The pain may go away when you take an aspirin, but that doesn't mean you've fixed the underlying problem. It's too bad that it often takes a crisis before we get help and discover the true status of our health.

"The same is true in business," I said. "Things may be going okay, but that doesn't mean your department or team is operating as well as it should be. Know your department's vital signs and monitor them for indications of an impending crisis. It shouldn't require almost getting fired for a leader to wake up and pay attention to his team's health."

Tom nodded. "Isn't that the truth. You're lucky that Carmen and the company cared enough to give you a second chance to improve your performance. I have a friend at another company who just got canned out of the blue."

"Yes, I'm grateful that Carmen was open to seeing the changes I wanted to make and that she was willing to give me time to implement them.

"I think my second takeaway from all of this," I continued, "is that it's critical to get checkups. Lynda and I have made it part of our family's routine. Everyone – Lynda, the kids and I – will get an annual checkup; every five or six years just isn't often enough.

"The same thing needs to happen in business," I said. "At regular intervals, leaders should stop, assess the condition of the team, interpret the metrics, diagnose any problems, and take action to fix those problems. If more people and more businesses would do those two things – pay attention to warning signs and get regular checkups – they could avoid the surprises and challenges that I faced."

"Those are good observations, Mike. Sounds like you've successfully turned a crisis into a learning experience."

"I really hope so, Tom. I don't want to have to go through that again," I said. "I've also learned that for long-term health and long-term success as a leader, you have to develop a plan, stick to it, and periodically measure your progress. You've got to know your vital signs and check them regularly. You have to have discipline and routines. And if you want lasting change, you're going to have to create new habits."

"You know those parallels you and I came up with in the hospital – the ones between the human body and an organization?" asked Tom. "I thought those were so powerful that I started using them with my team. They serve as a great reminder that all the parts of the organization are connected and interdependent. If one part isn't working well, it affects all the others."

"Yeah, my team and I have had great success with it too." I paused for a moment. "But I'd have to say that the biggest thing I've discovered is this: There *will be* more problems. Inevitably, there will be more health problems down the road and there will be more problems at work. There's no escaping it – it's a fact of life. The question is, are you going to be proactive and take action to avert a crisis, or are you going to do nothing and hope things turn out okay? It makes much more sense to be proactive about your health and your team's health. In the end, you'll spend less time preventing problems than you would fixing them. That old adage is true: an ounce of prevention really is worth a pound of cure.

"Because the real kicker is this: *you don't know when the crisis will happen.* When will those nagging symptoms develop into a health crisis? When will that frustrating situation at work reach the crisis point? No one knows. It could be tomorrow or next year or 12 years from now. So, *act now* to prevent a crisis. Don't wait for the wake-up call because not everyone gets a second chance."

Tom had been listening thoughtfully. "So why do you think people aren't more proactive about their health and about problems at work?"

I had to think about that for a minute. "*Knowing* something is one thing; but *doing* it is totally different. We all know it's important to do certain things – like exercising and eating well, or building trust and communicating effectively – but taking action is much harder. I know firsthand how hard it is to break out of a comfortable routine and break bad habits. For most people, there simply isn't enough urgency to overcome the inertia…that is, until the wake-up call comes.

"I think also that people are afraid to take responsibility because they might fail. And I think people make failure out to be a much bigger deal than it really is. Bottom line, it all comes down to you. You have to be accountable for the health of your body and the health of your team. You can, and should, solicit other people's help; but it's still ultimately up to you. You are the only one that can do what it takes to get and stay healthy. It just takes guts."

"I hear you," Tom agreed.

"So, knowing that there's always the potential for a crisis in the future and knowing how difficult it is for me to overcome my old habits, I wrote down some 'rules' to help me be proactive about my health – personal and business. I keep them posted near my computer so I'll see them often, and I carry this copy in my wallet." I handed him the little card I had pulled out.

> 1. *Accept responsibility for the problem…don't be in denial.*
> 2. *Recognize the warning signs and diagnose the problem early. Don't be afraid to find out what's really wrong. Get the checkup, run the tests, interpret the results.*
> 3. *Seek expert advice if necessary to help diagnose the problem and develop the appropriate strategy to cure the problem.*
> 4. *Take action!*

"There – now I think I'm done. How was that for an answer? A bit long-winded, eh?" I laughed.

"Not at all!" Tom said. "Experience is the best teacher. And you've certainly come out of your experience much stronger. I really like your rules – mind if I write them down for myself?"

"Please, take this copy. I'm happy to pass them along."

I glanced at my watch. "I should get going. I've got a lot to do before I leave."

"What's up?" asked Tom. "Business trip?"

"No. I've got a surprise for Lynda and the kids," I smiled a mischievous smile. "We're going on vacation – tomorrow morning!"

"Partner, you don't know how long I've waited to hear you say that. Good for you. Have a great time."

As we walked out of the restaurant, Tom put his hand on my shoulder and stopped me. He had a serious look on his face. "Hey, Mike – thanks for the great advice."

I smiled. For once I'd given more than I'd received. It was a great feeling.

■　　■　　■　　■　　■

When I walked in the front door at 1:30 in the afternoon, Lynda rushed up to me with a look of fear on her face. "Mike, what are you doing home? What's wrong? Are you okay?"

It was a hot summer day, and Josh and Rachel were inside playing. They must have heard the urgency in Lynda's voice, because they rushed out of the game room, alarm on their faces.

"Don't worry so much! I'm fine!" I laughed. "Pack your bags, everyone. We're going to the beach for a week! We leave first thing tomorrow morning!"

"What?!" said Josh.

"Really?" Rachel squealed with excitement.

"Yes, really. We're going on vacation...all of us. I've taken care of everything. All you have to do is pack your suitcases!"

"Oh, Mike!" Lynda ran to hug me and started to cry.

It was, without a doubt, the best day I had experienced in many years.

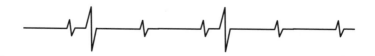

EPILOGUE

This is your wake-up call.

I hope that after reading *Leadership ER*, you have decided to be proactive and do some things differently in your life to avoid a future crisis and the need for an Emergency Room intervention.

But just making a decision changes nothing. Success in treating personal and professional ills is a matter of timely action:

Early **R**esponse

leads to

Easier **R**esolutions

that result in

Enormous **R**ewards.

Inevitably, there will be problems down the road in your personal and professional lives. More than likely, they will not be the same problems Mike experienced. Your health and business challenges will be unique to you and your situation. But the process for resolving them is the same nonetheless.

This book will be a success if you – and those you love – take the necessary steps to ensure long-term health. None of us knows if or when the crisis will happen. The real prescription for success is to *act now*…because not everyone gets a second chance.

About the Author

Stephen Krempl is an international speaker and trainer. He has led corporate training and education for Fortune 500 companies such as YUM! Brands, Inc., PepsiCo, and Motorola, and for the largest training and educational institute in Singapore. His 20-plus years in the field have provided him the opportunity to work with and train leaders at all levels in 25 countries.

He speaks regularly at local and national association conferences, public seminars, and organizational meetings around the world on topics ranging from change and process improvement to solving complex business problems. His unique and engaging presentation style is the result of his many years in training and his involvement in various aspects of stage, video, and television production.

Stephen is co-author of *Training Across Multiple Locations* (2001, Berrett-Koehler Publishers, Inc.) and *Business ER* (2003, Xulon Press) and has developed numerous training programs.

He is also an inventor. Drawing on his experiences as a speaker and trainer, he developed a new presentation theory that led to the development of new software and hardware that allows one person to easily run a multi-media presentation, thereby increasing the interest, retention and recall of any message.

Stephen appeared in the *International Who's Who* in 2000 and is a member of the American Society for Training and Development (ASTD), the National Speakers Association (NSA) and the Asian Regional Training and Development Organization (ARTDO).

Other CornerStone Leadership Books

Passionate Performance: Engaging Minds and Hearts to Conquer the Competition is a quick read offering practical strategies to engage the minds and hearts of your team at home, work, church or community. Learn why this is such a powerful advantage for your organization. Read it and conquer your competition! **$9.95**

Sticking to It: The Art of Adherence by Lee J. Colan reveals the secrets to success for high-achieving individuals and teams. It offers practical steps to help you consistently execute your plans. Read it and WIN! **$9.95**

Monday Morning Leadership is David Cottrell's best-selling book. It offers unique encouragement and direction that will help you become a better manager, employee, and person. **$12.95**
Monday Morning Leadership Audio CD **$19.95**

Management Insights explores the myths and realities of management. It provides insight into how you can become a successful manager. **$14.95**

The Manager's Communication Handbook is a powerful handbook that will help you connect with employees and create the understanding, support and acceptance critical to your success. **$9.95**

The Manager's Coaching Handbook is a practical guide to improving performance from your superstars, middle stars and falling stars. **$9.95**

175 Ways to Get More Done in Less Time has 175 excellent tips and techniques to help you get things done faster…and better. **$9.95**

Becoming the Obvious Choice is a roadmap showing employees how they can maintain their motivation, develop their hidden talents, and become the best. **$9.95**

180 Ways to Walk the Recognition Talk is packed with proven techniques and practical strategies that will help you encourage positive, productive performance. **$9.95**

136 Effective Presentation Tips is a powerful handbook providing 136 practical, easy-to-use tips to make every presentation a success. **$9.95**

Listen Up, Leader! Ever wonder what employees think about their leaders? This book tells you the seven characteristics of leadership that people will follow. **$9.95**

Visit www.**cornerstoneleadership**.com
for additional books and resources.

☑ **YES! Please send me extra copies of *Leadership ER!***
1-30 copies $14.95   31-100 copies $13.95   100+ copies $12.95

Leadership ER   ____ copies X _____   = $ _____

Additional Leadership Development Resources

Passionate Performance   ____ copies X $9.95   = $ _____

Sticking to It: The Art of Adherence   ____ copies X $9.95   = $ _____

Monday Morning Leadership   ____ copies X $12.95   = $ _____

Monday Morning Leadership Audio CD   ____ copies X $19.95   = $ _____

Management Insights   ____ copies X $14.95   = $ _____

The Manager's Communication Handbook   ____ copies X $9.95   = $ _____

The Manager's Coaching Handbook   ____ copies X $9.95   = $ _____

175 Ways to Get More Done in Less Time   ____ copies X $9.95   = $ _____

Becoming the Obvious Choice   ____ copies X $9.95   = $ _____

180 Ways to Walk the Recognition Talk   ____ copies X $9.95   = $ _____

136 Effective Presentation Tips   ____ copies X $9.95   = $ _____

Listen Up, Leader!   ____ copies X $9.95   = $ _____

Leader's Performance Package   ____ packs X $129.95   = $ _____
   (one of each of the items above,
   except Leadership ER)

Shipping & Handling $ _____

Subtotal $ _____

Sales Tax (8.25%-TX Only) $ _____

Total (U.S. Dollars Only) $ _____

Shipping and Handling Charges

Total $ Amount	Up to $49	$50-$99	$100-$249	$250-$1199	$1200-$2999	$3000+
Charge	$6	$9	$16	$30	$80	$125

Name _____ Job Title _____

Organization _____ Phone _____

Shipping Address _____ Fax _____

Billing Address _____ Email _____

City _____ State _____ Zip _____

❏ Please invoice (Orders over $200) Purchase Order Number (if applicable) _____

Charge Your Order: ❏ MasterCard   ❏ Visa   ❏ American Express

Credit Card Number _____ Exp. Date _____

Signature _____

❏ Check Enclosed (Payable to CornerStone Leadership)

Fax	Mail	Phone
972.274.2884	**P.O. Box 764087** **Dallas, TX 75376**	**888.789.5323**

www.cornerstoneleadership.com

CornerStone
Leadership Institute